The Constitution of Japan

装幀 ● 菊地　信義
装画 ● 野村　俊夫

図版キャプション（第1部）● 高橋　仁（スウェーデン社会研究所研究員）
解説（第2部）● Theodore H. McNelly（メリーランド大学名誉教授）

翻訳（第2部解説）● 高橋　豊子

本書の編集にあたっては、以下の方針を定めた。

1．「日本国憲法」及び「日本国憲法英訳文」は、『現行法規総覧』（衆議院法制局・参議院法制局編、第一法規出版刊行）に基づいた。

2．原典の「日本国憲法」は、歴史的かなづかいで、ルビはふられていないが、読みの難解なもの、特殊な読みをするもの等には、編集部の判断でルビをふった。ただし、ルビは、現代かなづかいとした。また、原典の「日本国憲法」は旧漢字を使用しているが、新漢字に置き換えた。

3．原典の「日本国憲法」の各条文には、項番号がふられていないが、便宜を考えて、2項以降には、項番号をふった。

4．条文部分に加えた語句の意味は、講談社刊行『日本語大辞典第2版』より、必要と思われる部分を引用した。

5．本書では、原則として、敬称は省略した。

Published by Kodansha International Ltd.,
17-14, Otowa 1-chome, Bunkyo-ku, Tokyo 112.

First edition 1997

ISBN4-7700-2191-7
97 98 99 10 9 8 7 6 5 4 3 2 1

ビジュアル
英語で読む日本国憲法
The Constitution of Japan

英文日本大百科事典［編］

Bilingual **B**ooks

まえがき

　本書は、「日本国憲法」施行50周年を記念して企画したものです。日本国憲法は日本の基本構造を定めた国家の基本法です。しかし、日常生活の中で憲法を手にする機会がある方は、そう多くはないようです。そういった方々にも、今一度「日本国憲法」を手にとっていただけるよう、親しみやすく、わかりやすいものになるよう心がけました。

　本書には、憲法に関連した日本の様々な断片を伝える写真を添えました。これらの写真により、憲法に親近感を抱いていただくとともに、戦後半世紀をふりかえっていただければさいわいです。

　本書には英語訳も添えました。英語で読むと、日本語で読んでいた時には気が付かなかったことが意外に出てくるのに、驚くことがあります。「日本語で読む」、「英語で読む」、「バイリンガルで読む」、乗り換え自由のお好きな読み方でお楽しみ下さい。

　「日本国憲法はアメリカからの押しつけだ」と言われることも多いようです。本書の第2部に付した解説は、『英文日本大百科事典』から引用したものですが、この解説は、GHQでの勤務経験もあるアメリカの比較政治学者、マックネリー博士が執筆したものです。日本国憲法の成立過程と特徴が、簡潔にまとめられています。アメリカ人の手によるこの解説を読むことにより、日本国憲法を、外国人の視点でふり返ることも出来ましょう。

　なお、本書の出版に際しては、青山学院大学の清水英夫名誉教授、広島大学の筑間正泰教授のお世話になりました。改めて感謝申し上げます。

講談社バイリンガル・ブックス編集部

PREFACE

This book commemorates the 50th anniversary of the Constitution of Japan, which has served as Japan's basic law for the latter half of the 20th century. Since many people do not seem to have the chance to review the Constitution once they leave school, this book is intended to offer such an opportunity.

A variety of photographs highlighting aspects of the Constitution accompanies the text. It is our hope that the text and accompanying photographs whet readers' interest in how the Constitution has guided Japan since the end of World War II.

The text also appears in English. Readers thus have the choice of enjoying the book in either Japanese or English, or switching from one language to the other. By reading the English version, we can appreciate elements of the Constitution that are not as visible when reading in our own language.

It is often said that the Constitution of Japan was "imposed on Japan by the United States." Part II of this book, which is an extract from the *Kodansha Encyclopedia of Japan*, was written by the American scholar, Dr. Theodore H. McNelly, who worked for General Douglas MacArthur's Headquarters in Tōkyō. Through his text, readers can learn about the Constitution from a bicultural perspective.

The editors would like to thank Professor Emeritus Shimizu Hideo of Aoyama Gakuin University and Professor Chikuma Masayoshi of Hiroshima University for their generous support of this publication.

Editorial Department for Kodansha Bilingual Books

目　次

CONTENTS

第1部・日本国憲法

Part I・The Constitution of Japan

朕は、日本国民の総意に基いて、新日本建設の礎が、定まるに至つたことを、深くよろこび、枢密顧問の諮詢及び帝国憲法第73条による帝国議会の議決を経た帝国憲法の改正を裁可し、ここにこれを公布せしめる。

御名御璽

昭和21年11月3日

内閣総理大臣兼 外 務 大 臣		吉田　　茂
国 務 大 臣	男爵	幣原喜重郎
司 法 大 臣		木村篤太郎
内 務 大 臣		大村　清一
文 部 大 臣		田中耕太郎
農 林 大 臣		和田　博雄
国 務 大 臣		斎藤　隆夫
逓 信 大 臣		一松　定吉
商 工 大 臣		星島　二郎
厚 生 大 臣		河合　良成
国 務 大 臣		植原悦二郎
運 輸 大 臣		平塚常次郎
大 蔵 大 臣		石橋　湛山
国 務 大 臣		金森徳次郎
国 務 大 臣		膳　桂之助

I rejoice that the foundation for the construction of a new Japan has been laid according to the will of the Japanese people, and hereby sanction and promulgate the amendments of the Imperial Japanese Constitution effected following the consultation with the Privy Council and the decision of the Imperial Diet made in accordance with Article 73 of the said Constitution.

Signed: HIROHITO, Seal of the Emperor

This third day of the eleventh month of the twenty-first year of Showa (November 3, 1946)

Countersigned:

Prime Minister and concurrently Minister for Foreign Affairs	YOSHIDA Shigeru
Minister of State	Baron SHIDEHARA Kijuro
Minister of Justice	KIMURA Tokutaro
Minister for Home Affairs	OMURA Seiichi
Minister of Education	TANAKA Kotaro
Minister of Agriculture and Forestry	WADA Hiroo
Minister of State	SAITO Takao
Minister of Communications	HITOTSUMATSU Sadayoshi
Minister of Commerce and Industry	HOSHIJIMA Niro
Minister of Welfare	KAWAI Yoshinari
Minister of State	UEHARA Etsujiro
Minister of Transportation	HIRATSUKA Tsunejiro
Minister of Finance	ISHIBASHI Tanzan
Minister of State	KANAMORI Tokujiro
Minister of State	ZEN Keinosuke

1946年（昭和21年）。太平洋戦争の敗戦か
ら1年あまり、歴史書や教科書に名称の
載らない革命が日本でおきた。全体主義
から民主主義へ、帝国主義から国際協調
と平和主義への価値観の逆転。この革命
は大日本帝国憲法を改正し、日本国憲法
を裁可することで成立した。（写真は日本
国憲法の公布書）。──写真・共同通信社

1946 About a year after the end of
World War Ⅱ, a revolution took place
in Japan. This revolution isn't named
in history books or text books. It
was a revolution of values: from total-
itarianism to democracy, from imperi-
alism to international cooperation
and peace. Replacing the Constitution of the Empire of Japan with the
current Constitution of Japan facili-
tated this revolution. (Picture shows
the Constitution of Japan.)

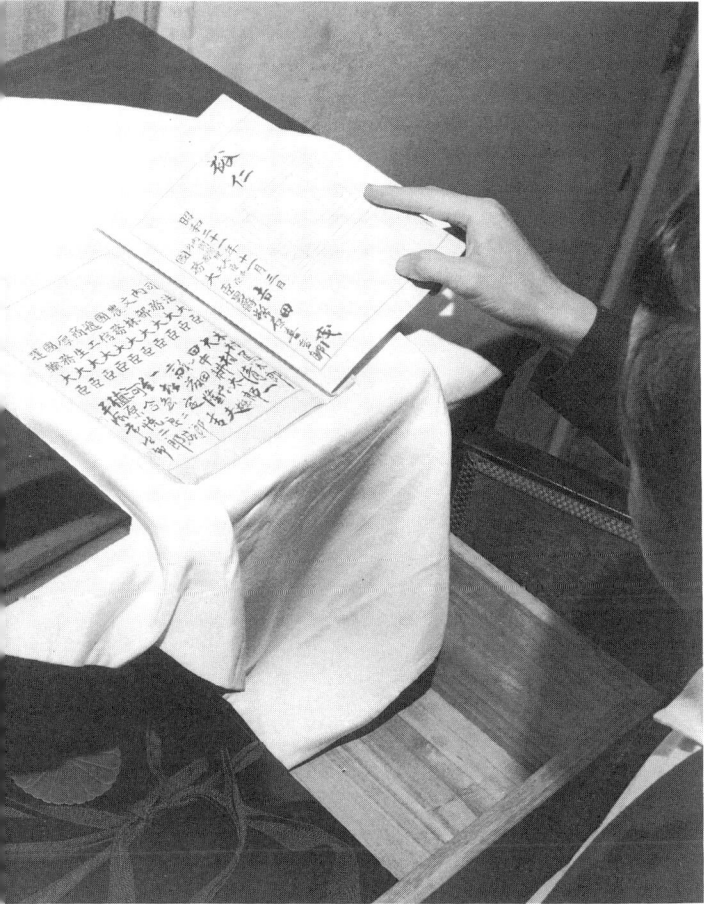

日本国憲法

日本国民は、正当に選挙された国会における代表者を通じて行動し、われらとわれらの子孫のために、諸国民との協和による成果と、わが国全土にわたつて自由のもたらす恵沢を確保し、政府の行為によつて再び戦争の惨禍が起ることのないやうにすることを決意し、ここに主権が国民に存することを宣言し、この憲法を確定する。そもそも国政は、国民の厳粛な信託によるものであつて、その権威は国民に由来し、その権力は国民の代表者がこれを行使し、その福利は国民がこれを享受する。これは人類普遍の原理であり、この憲法は、かかる原理に基くものである。われらは、これに反する一切の憲法、法令及び詔勅を排除する。

法　令：法律と命令。ひろくは条例・規則その他の法律形式を含んで、国法に属するすべての法に用いられる。

詔　勅：天皇が意思を表明する文書。詔書と勅語。みことのり。

日本国民は、恒久の平和を念願し、人間相互の関係を支配する崇高な理想を深く自覚するのであつて、平和を愛する諸国民の公正と信義に信頼して、われらの安全と生存を保持しようと決意した。われらは、平和を維持し、専制と隷従、圧迫と偏狭を地上から永遠に除去しようと努めてゐる国際社会において、名誉ある地位を占めたいと思ふ。われらは、全世界の国民が、ひとしく恐怖と欠乏から免かれ、平和のうちに生存する権利を有することを確認する。

THE CONSTITUTION OF JAPAN

We, the Japanese people, acting through our duly elected representatives in the National Diet, determined that we shall secure for ourselves and our posterity the fruits of peaceful cooperation with all nations and the blessings of liberty throughout this land, and resolved that never again shall we be visited with the horrors of war through the action of government, do proclaim that sovereign power resides with the people and do firmly establish this Constitution. Government is a sacred trust of the people, the authority for which is derived from the people, the powers of which are exercised by the representatives of the people, and the benefits of which are enjoyed by the people. This is a universal principle of mankind upon which this Constitution is founded. We reject and revoke all constitutions, laws, ordinances, and rescripts in conflict herewith.

We, the Japanese people, desire peace for all time and are deeply conscious of the high ideals controlling human relationship, and we have determined to preserve our security and existence, trusting in the justice and faith of the peace-loving peoples of the world. We desire to occupy an honored place in an international society striving for the preservation of peace, and the banishment of tyranny and slavery, oppression and intolerance for all time from the earth. We recognize that all peoples of the world have the right to live in

　われらは、いづれの国家も、自国のことのみに専念して他国を無視してはならないのであつて、政治道徳の法則は、普遍的なものであり、この法則に従ふことは、自国の主権を維持し、他国と対等関係に立たうとする各国の責務_{せきむ}であると信ずる。

　日本国民は、国家の名誉にかけ、全力をあげてこの崇高な理想と目的を達成することを誓_{ちか}ふ。

peace, free from fear and want.

We believe that no nation is responsible to itself alone, but that laws of political morality are universal; and that obedience to such laws is incumbent upon all nations who would sustain their own sovereignty and justify their sovereign relationship with other nations.

We, the Japanese people, pledge our national honor to accomplish these high ideals and purposes with all our resources.

18

1945年（昭和20年）。この年の8月15日の正午、ラジオで敗戦を告げる天皇の声を聞いた人々は、この皇居前広場でひれ伏し涙した。時は流れたが、この場所は往時の影を留める。

1945 At noon on 15 August, the Emperor announced Japan's unconditional surrender over the radio. Crowds gathered at the grounds of the Imperial Palace and fell to their knees. Times have changed, but this part of Tōkyō looks much the way it did decades ago.

第1章　天皇

第1条
　天皇は、日本国の象徴であり日本国民統合の象徴であつて、この地位は、主権の存する日本国民の総意に基く。

第2条
　皇位は、世襲のものであつて、国会の議決した皇室典範の定めるところにより、これを継承する。

第3条
　天皇の国事に関するすべての行為には、内閣の助言と承認を必要とし、内閣が、その責任を負ふ。

第4条
　天皇は、この憲法の定める国事に関する行為のみを行ひ、国政に関する権能を有しない。

　②天皇は、法律の定めるところにより、その国事に関する行為を委任することができる。

皇　位：天皇の地位。
皇室典範：皇位継承など、皇室に関する重要事項について定めた法律。昭和22年（1947）公布。

Chapter I THE EMPEROR

Article 1

The Emperor shall be the symbol of the State and of the unity of the people, deriving his position from the will of the people with whom resides sovereign power.

Article 2

The Imperial Throne shall be dynastic and succeeded to in accordance with the Imperial House Law passed by the Diet.

Article 3

The advice and approval of the Cabinet shall be required for all acts of the Emperor in matters of state, and the Cabinet shall be responsible therefor.

Article 4

The Emperor shall perform only such acts in matters of state as are provided for in this Constitution and he shall not have powers related to government.

(2) The Emperor may delegate the performance of his acts in matters of state as may be provided by law.

1946年（昭和21年）。この年の元旦、人間宣言を発した天皇は、国家の統治者から象徴になる。その後 8 年の歳月を費やし全国を行脚。昨日までの現人神を、国民は惑いながらも、熱狂的に歓迎。
　　　　　　　　　　　　　　　　　　　　　——写真・毎日新聞社

1946 On 1 January, the Emperor declared to the Japanese people that he was a man, not a god. Instead of divine ruler, he was now a symbol. Over the next eight years, he traveled throughout the country. The masses welcomed the Emperor, the former god, with some hesitation.

摂　政：君主にかわっ
て政務をとること。ま
た、その職や人。聖徳
太子以来皇族が任ぜら
れたが、清和天皇のと
き、外戚の藤原良房が
任命されてのち藤原氏
が就任。皇室典範には
天皇の未成年・病気・
事故のさいに、成年の
皇族をおくことが定め
られている。

第5条

　皇室典範の定めるところにより摂政を置くと
きは、摂政は、天皇の名でその国事に関する行
為を行ふ。この場合には、前条第1項の規定を
準用する。

第6条

　天皇は、国会の指名に基いて、内閣総理大臣
を任命する。

　②天皇は、内閣の指名に基いて、最高裁判所
の長たる裁判官を任命する。

第7条

　天皇は、内閣の助言と承認により、国民のた
めに、左の国事に関する行為を行ふ。

1　憲法改正、法律、政令及び条約を公布す
　　ること。
2　国会を召集すること。
3　衆議院を解散すること。
4　国会議員の総選挙の施行を公示すること。

5　国務大臣及び法律の定めるその他の官吏
　　の任免並びに全権委任状及び大使及び公
　　使の信任状を認証すること。

Article 5

When, in accordance with the Imperial House Law, a Regency is established, the Regent shall perform his acts in matters of state in the Emperor's name. In this case, paragraph one of the preceding article will be applicable.

Article 6

The Emperor shall appoint the Prime Minister as designated by the Diet.

(2) The Emperor shall appoint the Chief Judge of the Supreme Court as designated by the Cabinet.

Article 7

The Emperor, with the advice and approval of the Cabinet, shall perform the following acts in matters of state on behalf of the people:

(i) Promulgation of amendments of the constitution, laws, cabinet orders and treaties;

(ii) Convocation of the Diet;

(iii) Dissolution of the House of Representatives;

(iv) Proclamation of general election of members of the Diet;

(v) Attestation of the appointment and dismissal of Ministers of State and other officials as provided for by law, and of full powers and credentials of Ambassadors and Ministers;

1947年（昭和22年）。新憲法下での第1回目の国会開会式は、天皇
陛下のご出席を仰いで、この年の6月23日に行われた。松岡駒吉
衆議院議長は、陛下にうしろを見せて式辞を述べる。国会の召集
は、憲法第7条に基づく、天皇の国事行為である。

1947 The first Diet opening ceremony under the new
Constitution was held on 23 June. Matsuoka Komakichi,
Speaker of the House of Representatives, delivered his
opening address with his back to the Emperor. Per
Article 7 of the Constitution, the Emperor convenes the
Diet with the advice and approval of the Cabinet.

大　赦：恩赦の1つ。
政令で定めた罪につい
て、有罪の言い渡しを
うけた者についてはそ
の言い渡しの効力を、
まだその言い渡しをう
けていない者について
は公訴権を消滅させる
もの。

特　赦：恩赦の1つ。
有罪の言い渡しを受け
た特定の者に対し、刑
の執行を免除し、有罪
言い渡しの効力を失わ
せること。

減　刑：恩赦の1つ。
確定している刑または
刑の執行を軽くするこ
と。罪または刑の種類
を定めて行うものと、
特定の者に対して行う
ものとがある。

復　権：いったん失っ
た法律上の資格や権利
を回復させること。刑
法上・恩赦法上・破産
法上のものがある。

栄　典：①めでたい儀
式。②国家社会に功労
のあった者の栄誉を表
彰するために与えられ
る特別の地位。位階・
勲章など。

6　大赦、特赦、減刑、刑の執行の免除及び
　　復権を認証すること。

7　栄典を授与すること。

8　批准書及び法律の定めるその他の外交
　　文書を認証すること。

9　外国の大使及び公使を接受すること。

10　儀式を行ふこと。

第8条

　皇室に財産を譲り渡し、又は皇室が、財産を
譲り受け、若しくは賜与することは、国会の議
決に基かなければならない。

(vi) Attestation of general and special amnesty, commutation of punishment, reprieve, and restoration of rights;

(vii) Awarding of honors;

(viii) Attestation of instruments of ratification and other diplomatic documents as provided for by law;

(ix) Receiving foreign ambassadors and ministers;

(x) Performance of ceremonial functions.

Article 8

No property can be given to, or received by, the Imperial House, nor can any gifts be made therefrom, without the authorization of the Diet.

1959年（昭和34年）。皇太子ご成婚。開
かれた皇室に、4月10日のご成婚の日
には、日本中がテレビにクギづけ。中
継のアナウンサーは民間出身のお妃を、
「美智子さん」と「さん」づけで呼んだ。
皇太子妃のニックネームにあやかった
「ミッチーブーム」は、日本でテレビが
普及する大きなきっかけとなった
——写真・朝日新聞社

1959 The Crown Prince married a
commoner on 10 April. That day,
Japanese eyes were glued to the
television. Television reporters called her Michiko-*san* instead of the
honorific term Michiko-*sama*. The
"Michy boom" spurred television
sales.

第2章　戦争の放棄

第9条

　日本国民は、正義と秩序を基調とする国際平和を誠実に希求し、国権の発動たる戦争と、武力による威嚇又は武力の行使は、国際紛争を解決する手段としては、永久にこれを放棄する。

　②前項の目的を達するため、陸海空軍その他の戦力は、これを保持しない。国の交戦権は、これを認めない。

Chapter II RENUNCIATION OF WAR

Article 9

Aspiring sincerely to an international peace based on justice and order, the Japanese people forever renounce war as a sovereign right of the nation and the threat or use of force as means of settling international disputes.

(2) In order to accomplish the aim of the preceding paragraph, land, sea, and air forces, as well as other war potential, will never be maintained. The right of belligerency of the state will not be recognized.

1945年（昭和20年）。憲法草案の作成
に携わったある米国人は、「日本国憲
法は悲惨な戦禍から生まれた真珠」と
評した。また、「日本を再び戦場にす
るな」という日本人の願いは、憲法第
9条への圧倒的支持となって表れた。
ここ銀座4丁目交差点付近は、時代ご
とに新しい装いをまといながら今日に
至っている。　　──撮影・菊池俊吉

1945 One of the Americans who
helped draft the postwar constitution said, "Japan's Constitution
is a pearl born from the tragedy
of war." The Japanese desire that
the country never again become
a battlefield was reflected in their
strong support of Article 9 in the
Constitution. The area around
Ginza's 4-chōme intersection con-
tinues to offer a modern face to
each new generation.

| 第3章 | 国民の権利及び義務 |

第10条

日本国民たる要件は、法律でこれを定める。

第11条

享　有：権利・能力な
どを、生まれながらに
もっていること。

国民は、すべての基本的人権の享有を妨げら
れない。この憲法が国民に保障する基本的人権
は、侵すことのできない永久の権利として、現
在及び将来の国民に与へられる。

第12条

この憲法が国民に保障する自由及び権利は、
国民の不断の努力によつて、これを保持しなけ
ればならない。又、国民は、これを濫用しては

福　祉：①さいわい。
幸福。②人々が幸福で
安定した暮らしができ
る環境。また、その実
現のための施策。

ならないのであつて、常に公共の福祉のために
これを利用する責任を負ふ。

第13条

すべて国民は、個人として尊重される。生命、
自由及び幸福追求に対する国民の権利について
は、公共の福祉に反しない限り、立法その他の
国政の上で、最大の尊重を必要とする。

CHAPTER III RIGHTS AND DUTIES OF THE PEOPLE

Article 10

The conditions necessary for being a Japanese national shall be determined by law.

Article 11

The people shall not be prevented from enjoying any of the fundamental human rights. These fundamental human rights guaranteed to the people by this Constitution shall be conferred upon the people of this and future generations as eternal and inviolate rights.

Article 12

The freedoms and rights guaranteed to the people by this Constitution shall be maintained by the constant endeavor of the people, who shall refrain from any abuse of these freedoms and rights and shall always be responsible for utilizing them for the public welfare.

Article 13

All of the people shall be respected as individuals. Their right to life, liberty, and the pursuit of happiness shall, to the extent that it does not interfere with the public welfare, be the supreme consideration in legislation and in other governmental affairs.

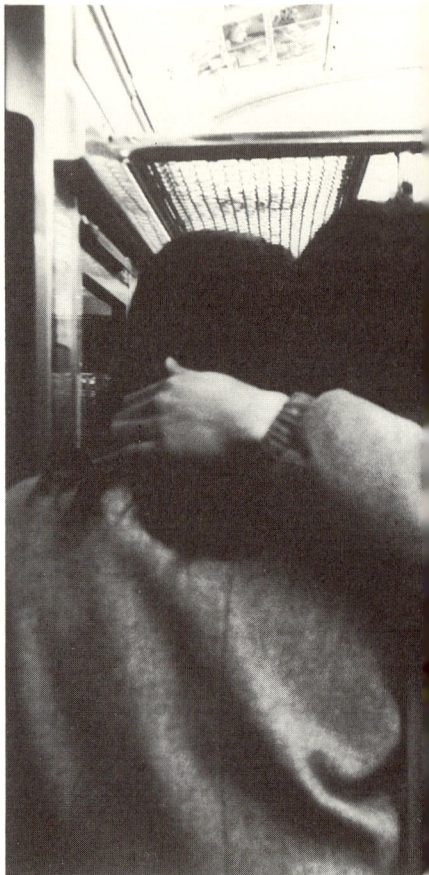

1997年（平成9年）。「キスする自由」もあれば「見せつけられる不快からの自由」もある。新憲法によって日本人は様々な自由を手にしたが、他方では幾種類もの自由が併存するようになった。日本国憲法は、自由や権利の尊重と歯止めの規準として、「公共の福祉」を用いている。　　　　　　　　——写真・真島写真事務所

1997 People are now free to kiss in public and they also have the freedom not to have to watch. The Constitution gives Japanese people many new types of freedoms. It balances respect for individual freedom and rights with the words "public welfare."

40

門　地：家柄。家格。
門閥。

華　族：明治2年
（1869）従来の公卿・
諸侯に与えられた族
称。同17年（1884）華
族令で公・侯・伯・
子・男の五爵が定めら
れ、国家に勲功ある者
もこれに列し、特権の
ある社会的身分となっ
た。昭和22年（1947）
廃止。

第14条

　すべて国民は、法の下に平等であつて、人種、信条、性別、社会的身分又は門地により、政治的、経済的又は社会的関係において、差別されない。

　②華族その他の貴族の制度は、これを認めない。

　③栄誉、勲章その他の栄典の授与は、いかなる特権も伴はない。栄典の授与は、現にこれを有し、又は将来これを受ける者の一代に限り、その効力を有する。

第15条

　公務員を選定し、及びこれを罷免することは、国民固有の権利である。

　②すべて公務員は、全体の奉仕者であつて、一部の奉仕者ではない。

　③公務員の選挙については、成年者による普通選挙を保障する。

　④すべて選挙における投票の秘密は、これを侵してはならない。選挙人は、その選択に関し公的にも私的にも責任を問はれない。

Article 14

All of the people are equal under the law and there shall be no discrimination in political, economic or social relations because of race, creed, sex, social status or family origin.

(2) Peers and peerage shall not be recognized.

(3) No privilege shall accompany any award of honor, decoration or any distinction, nor shall any such award be valid beyond the lifetime of the individual who now holds or hereafter may receive it.

Article 15

The people have the inalienable right to choose their public officials and to dismiss them.

(2) All public officials are servants of the whole community and not of any group thereof.

(3) Universal adult suffrage is guaranteed with regard to the election of public officials.

(4) In all elections, secrecy of the ballot shall not be violated. A voter shall not be answerable, publicly or privately for the choice he has made.

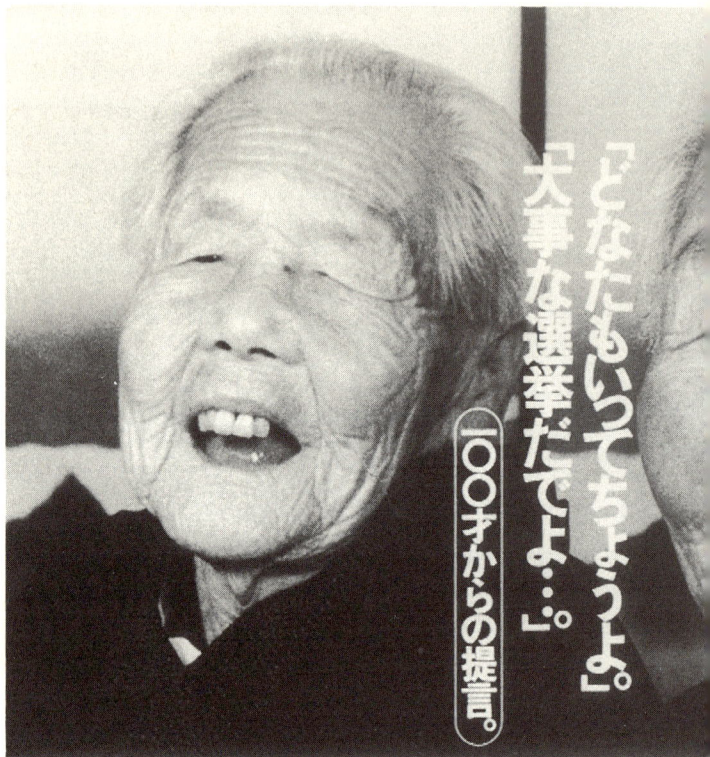

「どなたもいってちょうよ」。
「大事な選挙だでよ‥‥」。

一〇〇才からの提言。

明るい選挙、私たちの暮らしと政治について
身近なところから、話し合ってみませんか。

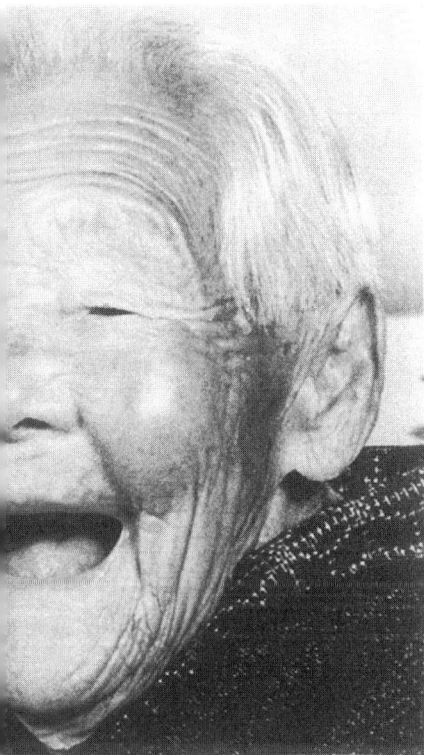

政治家の寄附は 禁止されています。
● 贈らない ● 求めない ● 受けとらない。

名古屋市・区選挙管理委員会　明るい選挙名古屋市・区推進協議会

1992年（平成4年）。2人合わせて200
歳を越すきんさんとぎんさん姉妹。彼
女たちの人生の前半を占める戦前に
は、選挙権はなく、政党に加入するこ
とも出来なかった。昭和の女性解放運
動のリーダー故市川房枝参議院議員
は、若い女性に常に言ったという、
「権利の上に眠るな」と。（写真は1992
年の参議院選挙ポスター）

1992 The combined age of sisters
Kin-san and Gin-san is more than
200. For the half of their lives
before World War II, they did not
have the right to vote or join political parties. Ichikawa Fusae, the
now deceased women's rights
leader and once member of the
House of Councillors, often told
young women, "Do not sleep on
your rights." (From a poster for
the 1992 House of Councillors'
election)

第16条

　何人も、損害の救済、公務員の罷免、法律、命令又は規則の制定、廃止又は改正その他の事項に関し、平穏に請願する権利を有し、何人も、かかる請願をしたためにいかなる差別待遇も受けない。

第17条

　何人も、公務員の不法行為により、損害を受けたときは、法律の定めるところにより、国又は公共団体に、その賠償を求めることができる。

第18条

　何人も、いかなる奴隷的拘束も受けない。又、犯罪に因る処罰の場合を除いては、その意に反する苦役に服させられない。

第19条

　思想及び良心の自由は、これを侵してはならない。

第20条

　信教の自由は、何人に対してもこれを保障する。いかなる宗教団体も、国から特権を受け、又は政治上の権力を行使してはならない。

　②何人も、宗教上の行為、祝典、儀式又は行事に参加することを強制されない。

Article 16

Every person shall have the right of peaceful petition for the redress of damage, for the removal of public officials, for the enactment, repeal or amendment of laws, ordinances or regulations and for other matters; nor shall any person be in any way discriminated against for sponsoring such a petition.

Article 17

Every person may sue for redress as provided by law from the State or a public entity, in case he has suffered damage through illegal act of any public official.

Article 18

No person shall be held in bondage of any kind. Involuntary servitude, except as punishment for crime, is prohibited.

Article 19

Freedom of thought and conscience shall not be violated.

Article 20

Freedom of religion is guaranteed to all. No religious organization shall receive any privileges from the State, nor exercise any political authority.

(2) No person shall be compelled to take part in any religious act, celebration, rite or practice.

1989年（平成元年）。この前年、自民党は税制改革関連6法案を強行採決し、消費税が1989年4月からスタートした。憲法第16条は、何人も請願する権利を有すると定めている。国民は様々なパフォーマンスをくりだし、国会になおもプレッシャーをかける。その年の7月に行われた参院選では、戦後常に多数を維持してきた自民党は大敗し、過半数割れ。これをきっかけとして与野党逆転現象が起こる。

1989 The Liberal Democratic Party forced the passage of laws to change the tax system in 1988, leading to the introduction of a consumption tax in April 1989. Article 16 of the Constitution states "every person shall have the right of peaceful petition for the enactment, repeal or amendment of laws." People protested against the new tax and put pressure on the Diet. In July, the LDP lost control of the Upper House for the first time since 1955, bringing the opposition parties to power.

48

③国及びその機関は、宗教教育その他いかなる宗教的活動もしてはならない。

第21条

集会、結社及び言論、出版その他一切の表現の自由は、これを保障する。

②検閲は、これをしてはならない。通信の秘密は、これを侵してはならない。

第22条

何人も、公共の福祉に反しない限り、居住、移転及び職業選択の自由を有する。

②何人も、外国に移住し、又は国籍を離脱する自由を侵されない。

第23条

学問の自由は、これを保障する。

第24条

婚姻は、両性の合意のみに基いて成立し、夫婦が同等の権利を有することを基本として、相互の協力により、維持されなければならない。

結 社：共同の目的をとげるため、複数の人間が継続的な集合をつくること。また、その組織。

検 閲：①調べあらためること。②言論統制の1つ。公権力が出版物・放送・映画などの内容を強制的に調べ、好ましくないものの公開を制限したり罰したりすること。

婚 姻：社会的に公認された男女の継続的な性的結合の制度。また、その結合を生じる契約。戸籍法に基づく届け出によって成立する。結婚。

(3) The State and its organs shall refrain from religious education or any other religious activity.

Article 21
Freedom of assembly and association as well as speech, press and all other forms of expression are guaranteed.

(2) No censorship shall be maintained, nor shall the secrecy of any means of communication be violated.

Article 22
Every person shall have freedom to choose and change his residence and to choose his occupation to the extent that it does not interfere with the public welfare.

(2) Freedom of all persons to move to a foreign country and to divest themselves of their nationality shall be inviolate.

Article 23
Academic freedom is guaranteed.

Article 24
Marriage shall be based only on the mutual consent of both sexes and it shall be maintained through mutual cooperation with the equal rights of husband and wife as a basis.

1953年（昭和28年）。この年の2月にNHKがテレビ放送を開始、民放もそれに続く。街頭に置かれたテレビは、まもなくお茶の間にも普及。言論、出版、表現の自由は、マスメディアの発達とともに日本に浸透するが、それに並行して、名誉毀損やプライバシー侵害の問題等、自由の弊害も目立ってきた。　　　　　──写真・読売ニュース写真

1953 In February, NHK, Japan's first television station, began broadcasting. Private television stations soon followed. People first watched televisions in store windows, but soon they were watching them in their own living rooms. The mass media helped promote the freedoms of speech, press and expression, and also brought to the forefront issues such as defamation of character and violation of privacy.

②配偶者の選択、財産権、相続、住居の選定、離婚並びに婚姻及び家族に関するその他の事項に関しては、法律は、個人の尊厳と両性の本質的平等に立脚して、制定されなければならない。

第25条

すべて国民は、健康で文化的な最低限度の生活を営む権利を有する。

②国は、すべての生活部面について、社会福祉、社会保障及び公衆衛生の向上及び増進に努めなければならない。

第26条

すべて国民は、法律の定めるところにより、その能力に応じて、ひとしく教育を受ける権利を有する。

②すべて国民は、法律の定めるところにより、その保護する子女に普通教育を受けさせる義務を負ふ。義務教育は、これを無償とする。

子 女：①むすことむすめ。子ども。②女の子

第27条

すべて国民は、勤労の権利を有し、義務を負ふ。

②賃金、就業時間、休息その他の勤労条件に関する基準は、法律でこれを定める。

③児童は、これを酷使してはならない。

(2) With regard to choice of spouse, property rights, inheritance, choice of domicile, divorce and other matters pertaining to marriage and the family, laws shall be enacted from the standpoint of individual dignity and the essential equality of the sexes.

Article 25

All people shall have the right to maintain the minimum standards of wholesome and cultured living.

(2) In all spheres of life, the State shall use its endeavors for the promotion and extension of social welfare and security, and of public health.

Article 26

All people shall have the right to receive an equal education correspondent to their ability, as provided by law.

(2) All people shall be obligated to have all boys and girls under their protection receive ordinary education as provided for by law. Such compulsory education shall be free.

Article 27

All people shall have the right and the obligation to work.

(2) Standards for wages, hours, rest and other working conditions shall be fixed by law.

(3) Children shall not be exploited.

1996年（平成 8 年）。巨大都市新宿、見上げれば高層ビル群、豊かな生活が広がる。だがその足元には、居場所を求めホームレスが集まる。憲法第25条にうたわれている「健康で文化的な最低限度の生活を営む権利」をめぐる葛藤がある。
——写真・共同通信社

1996 The Shinjuku city center is crowded with skyscrapers and other symbols of abundance. At the foot of these buildings, homeless people gather. Article 25 of the Constitution states, "All people shall have the right to maintain the minimum standards of wholesome and cultured living."

56

第28条

　勤労者の団結する権利及び団体交渉その他の団体行動をする権利は、これを保障する。

第29条

　財産権は、これを侵してはならない。

　②財産権の内容は、公共の福祉に適合するやうに、法律でこれを定める。

　③私有財産は、正当な補償の下に、これを公共のために用ひることができる。

第30条

　国民は、法律の定めるところにより、納税の義務を負ふ。

第31条

　何人も、法律の定める手続によらなければ、その生命若しくは自由を奪はれ、又はその他の刑罰を科せられない。

第32条

　何人も、裁判所において裁判を受ける権利を奪はれない。

第33条

　何人も、現行犯として逮捕される場合を除いては、権限を有する司法官憲が発し、且つ理由となつてゐる犯罪を明示する令状によらなければ、逮捕されない。

官　憲：①官庁の法規。②政府。役所。③官吏。警察官。

Article 28

The right of workers to organize and to bargain and act collectively is guaranteed.

Article 29

The right to own or to hold property is inviolable.

(2) Property rights shall be defined by law, in conformity with the public welfare.

(3) Private property may be taken for public use upon just compensation therefor.

Article 30

The people shall be liable to taxations as provided by law.

Article 31

No person shall be deprived of life or liberty, nor shall any other criminal penalty be imposed, except according to procedure established by law.

Article 32

No person shall be denied the right of access to the courts.

Article 33

No person shall be apprehended except upon warrant issued by a competent judicial officer which specifies the offense with which the person is charged, unless he is apprehended, the offense being committed.

58

1997年（平成9年）。街にあふれる勤労の機会と権利。必要な時には
いつでも気楽にアルバイト、定職を持たなくても良いのが今の
時代か。「大学は出たけれど就職口がない」と言われたのは、も
はや昔話だろうか……。　　　　　　　　──写真・真島写真事務所

1997 The city provides many different job opportunities.
When in need of money, there is a choice of full or part-
time work and people do not have to worry about their
future. Is "I have a college diploma but no job" now a
statement of yesteryear?

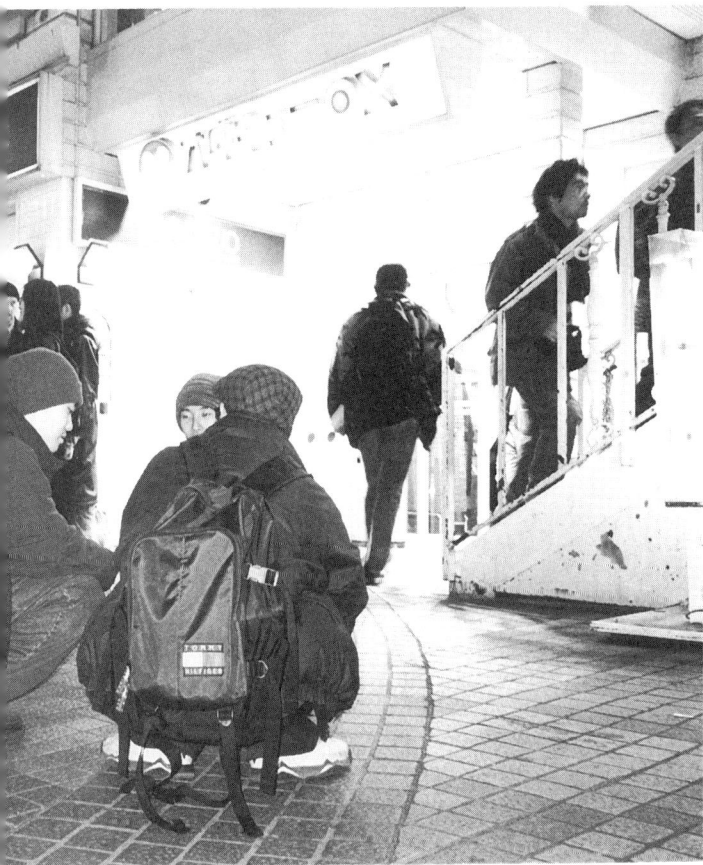

60

抑　留：①むりにひき
とめておくこと。②逮
捕に引き続いて、比較
的短期間、身柄を拘束
すること。③国際法上、
捕虜や物件、とくに船
舶などの自由な移動を
制限し、自国内のある
場所にとどめおくこ
と。

拘　禁：①つかまえて
とどめておくこと。②
留置所や刑務所などに
収容し、比較的長期に
わたって身体的自由を
拘束すること。

第34条

　何人も、理由を直ちに告げられ、且つ、直ち
に弁護人に依頼する権利を与へられなければ、
抑留又は拘禁されない。又、何人も、正当な理
由がなければ、拘禁されず、要求があれば、そ
の理由は、直ちに本人及びその弁護人の出席す
る公開の法廷で示されなければならない。

第35条

　何人も、その住居、書類及び所持品について、
侵入、捜索及び押収を受けることのない権利は、
第33条の場合を除いては、正当な理由に基いて
発せられ、且つ捜索する場所及び押収する物を
明示する令状がなければ、侵されない。

　②捜索又は押収は、権限を有する司法官憲が
発する各別の令状により、これを行ふ。

第36条

　公務員による拷問及び残虐な刑罰は、絶対に
これを禁ずる。

第37条

　すべて刑事事件においては、被告人は、公平
な裁判所の迅速な公開裁判を受ける権利を有す
る。

Article 34

No person shall be arrested or detained without being at once informed of the charges against him or without the immediate privilege of counsel; nor shall he be detained without adequate cause; and upon demand of any person such cause must be immediately shown in open court in his presence and the presence of his counsel.

Article 35

The right of all persons to be secure in their homes, papers and effects against entries, searches and seizures shall not be impaired except upon warrant issued for adequate cause and particularly describing the place to be searched and things to be seized, or except as provided by Article 33.

(2) Each search or seizure shall be made upon separate warrant issued by a competent judicial officer.

Article 36

The infliction of torture by any public officer and cruel punishments are absolutely forbidden.

Article 37

In all criminal cases the accused shall enjoy the right to a speedy and public trial by an impartial tribunal.

「現行犯で逮捕する」、「公務執行妨害で逮捕する」、「捜索令状です」。日本国憲法は、正当な理由がなければ逮捕や捜索をされないと保障している.
──絵・『天才バカボン』より　©フジオ・プロ

"I caught you in the act. You are under arrest." "I am arresting you for interfering with a public employee's duties." "I have a search warrant." The Constitution provides that people cannot be apprehended or searched without good cause.

審　問：①くわしく問いたずねること。②民事訴訟法上、裁判官が、口頭弁論の形式によらず、当事者などに個々に口頭または書面で陳述させること。

②刑事被告人は、すべての証人に対して審問する機会を充分に与へられ、又、公費で自己のために強制的手続により証人を求める権利を有する。

③刑事被告人は、いかなる場合にも、資格を有する弁護人を依頼することができる。被告人が自らこれを依頼することができないときは、国でこれを附する。

第38条

何人も、自己に不利益な供述を強要されない。

自　白：①自分で白状すること。②訴訟手続きで、被告人または被疑者が自分がなした犯罪事実を認める供述。③民事訴訟で、相手方が主張する自分に不利益な事実を認めること。また、その旨の陳述。

②強制、拷問若しくは脅迫による自白又は不当に長く抑留若しくは拘禁された後の自白は、これを証拠とすることができない。

③何人も、自己に不利益な唯一の証拠が本人の自白である場合には、有罪とされ、又は刑罰を科せられない。

第39条

何人も、実行の時に適法であつた行為又は既に無罪とされた行為については、刑事上の責任を問はれない。又、同一の犯罪について、重ねて刑事上の責任を問はれない。

第40条

何人も、抑留又は拘禁された後、無罪の裁判を受けたときは、法律の定めるところにより、国にその補償を求めることができる。

(2) He shall be permitted full opportunity to examine all witnesses, and he shall have the right of compulsory process for obtaining witnesses on his behalf at public expense.

(3) At all times the accused shall have the assistance of competent counsel who shall, if the accused is unable to secure the same by his own efforts, be assigned to his use by the State.

Article 38

No person shall be compelled to testify against himself.

(2) Confession made under compulsion, torture or threat, or after prolonged arrest or detention shall not be admitted in evidence.

(3) No person shall be convicted or punished in cases where the only proof against him is his own confession.

Article 39

No person shall be held criminally liable for an act which was lawful at the time it was committed, or of which he has been acquitted, nor shall he be placed in double jeopardy.

Article 40

Any person, in case he is acquitted after he has been arrested or detained, may sue the State for redress as provided by law.

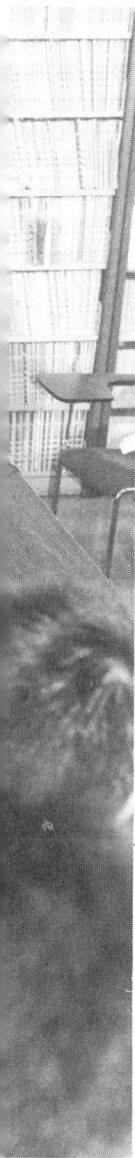

1995年（平成 7 年）。オウム真理教による戦後最大規模の無差別テロ事件。教団前代表松本智津夫（麻原彰晃）容疑者は、私選弁護人である横山昭二弁護士を、裁判の直前になって解任。結局、松本（麻原）被告には国選弁護人がついた。このドタバタ劇を、スキャンダルとして取り上げるメディアもあったが、資格を有する弁護人を依頼する権利は、憲法第37条で何人にも保障されている。

1995 The Aum Shinrikyō cult was behind the largest terrorist attack in postwar Japan. The cult leader, Asahara Shōkō, hired a lawyer, Yokoyama Shōji, but then fired him right before the start of the trial. He was then provided a state-assigned defense team. An accused's right to the "assistance of competent counsel" is guaranteed by Article 37 of the Constitution.

第4章　国　会

第41条

　国会は、国権（こっけん）の最高機関であつて、国の唯一の立法機関である。

第42条

　国会は、衆議院及び参議院の両議院でこれを構成する。

第43条

　両議院は、全国民を代表する選挙された議員でこれを組織する。

　②両議院の議員の定数（ていすう）は、法律でこれを定める。

第44条

　両議院の議員及びその選挙人の資格は、法律でこれを定める。但（ただ）し、人種、信条、性別、社会的身分、門地、教育、財産又は収入によつて差別してはならない。

第45条

　衆議院議員の任期は、４年とする。但し、衆議院解散の場合には、その期間満了前に終了する。

Chapter IV THE DIET

Article 41

The Diet shall be the highest organ of state power, and shall be the sole law-making organ of the State.

Article 42

The Diet shall consist of two Houses, namely the House of Representatives and the House of Councillors.

Article 43

Both Houses shall consist of elected members, representative of all the people.

(2) The number of the members of each House shall be fixed by law.

Article 44

The qualifications of members of both Houses and their electors shall be fixed by law. However, there shall be no discrimination because of race, creed, sex, social status, family origin, education, property or income.

Article 45

The term of office of members of the House of Representatives shall be four years. However, the term shall be terminated before the full term is up in case the House of Representatives is dissolved.

1946年（昭和21年）。議会警務課のきも入りで、昨年から少しずつ
始めたが、今日も昼時には職員達は議事堂畑で汗まみれ。今年は
さつまいも、麦、トマト、豆などを植えつけた。ちょうどその頃、
議事堂の中では、憲法の草案に関して熱い議論がなされていたの
だろうか。

1946 Sweet potatoes, wheat, tomatoes and beans were
popular items from the "Diet Garden". Diet clerks sweated in the garden during their lunch break, while politicians
sweated over the draft of the constitution.

72

第46条

　参議院議員の任期は、6年とし、3年ごとに議員の半数を改選する。

第47条

　選挙区、投票の方法その他両議院の議員の選挙に関する事項は、法律でこれを定める。

第48条

　何人も、同時に両議院の議員たることはできない。

第49条

　両議院の議員は、法律の定めるところにより、国庫から相当額の歳費を受ける。

第50条

　両議院の議員は、法律の定める場合を除いては、国会の会期中逮捕されず、会期前に逮捕された議員は、その議院の要求があれば、会期中これを釈放しなければならない。

Article 46

The term of office of members of the House of Councillors shall be six years, and election for half the members shall take place every three years.

Article 47

Electoral districts, method of voting and other matters pertaining to the method of election of members of both Houses shall be fixed by law.

Article 48

No person shall be permitted to be a member of both Houses simultaneously.

Article 49

Members of both Houses shall receive appropriate annual payment from the national treasury in accordance with law.

Article 50

Except in cases provided by law, members of both Houses shall be exempt from apprehension while the Diet is in session, and any members apprehended before the opening of the session shall be freed during the term of the session upon demand of the House.

1960年（昭和35年）。主権は国民にあるが、「国会は、国権の最高機関であつて、国の唯一の立法機関である」と、憲法第41条は規定している。6月18日、新日米安保条約の成立を阻止しようと、33万人の市民や学生が国会を包囲。が、この翌日自然承認される。——写真・朝日新聞社

1960 Although sovereign power resides with people, Article 41 of the Constitution says that the "Diet shall be the highest organ of state power, and shall be the sole law-making organ of the State." This massive demonstration at the National Diet on 18 June attracted some 330,000 people in an unsuccessful protest against the renewal of the US-Japan Security Treaty. The renewal was ratified the following day.

第51条

　両議院の議員は、議院で行つた演説、討論又は表決について、院外で責任を問はれない。

第52条

　国会の常会は、毎年1回これを召集する。

第53条

　内閣は、国会の臨時会の召集を決定することができる。いづれかの議院の総議員の4分の1以上の要求があれば、内閣は、その召集を決定しなければならない。

第54条

　衆議院が解散されたときは、解散の日から40日以内に、衆議院議員の総選挙を行ひ、その選挙の日から30日以内に、国会を召集しなければならない。

　②衆議院が解散されたときは、参議院は、同時に閉会となる。但し、内閣は、国に緊急の必要があるときは、参議院の緊急集会を求めることができる。

Article 51

Members of both Houses shall not be held liable outside the House for speeches, debates or votes cast inside the House.

Article 52

An ordinary session of the Diet shall be convoked once per year.

Article 53

The Cabinet may determine to convoke extraordinary sessions of the Diet. When a quarter or more of the total members of either House makes the demand, the Cabinet must determine on such convocation.

Article 54

When the House of Representatives is dissolved, there must be a general election of members of the House of Representatives within forty (40) days from the date of dissolution, and the Diet must be convoked within thirty (30) days from the date of the election.

(2) When the House of Representatives is dissolved, the House of Councillors is closed at the same time. However, the Cabinet may in time of national emergency convoke the House of Councillors in emergency session.

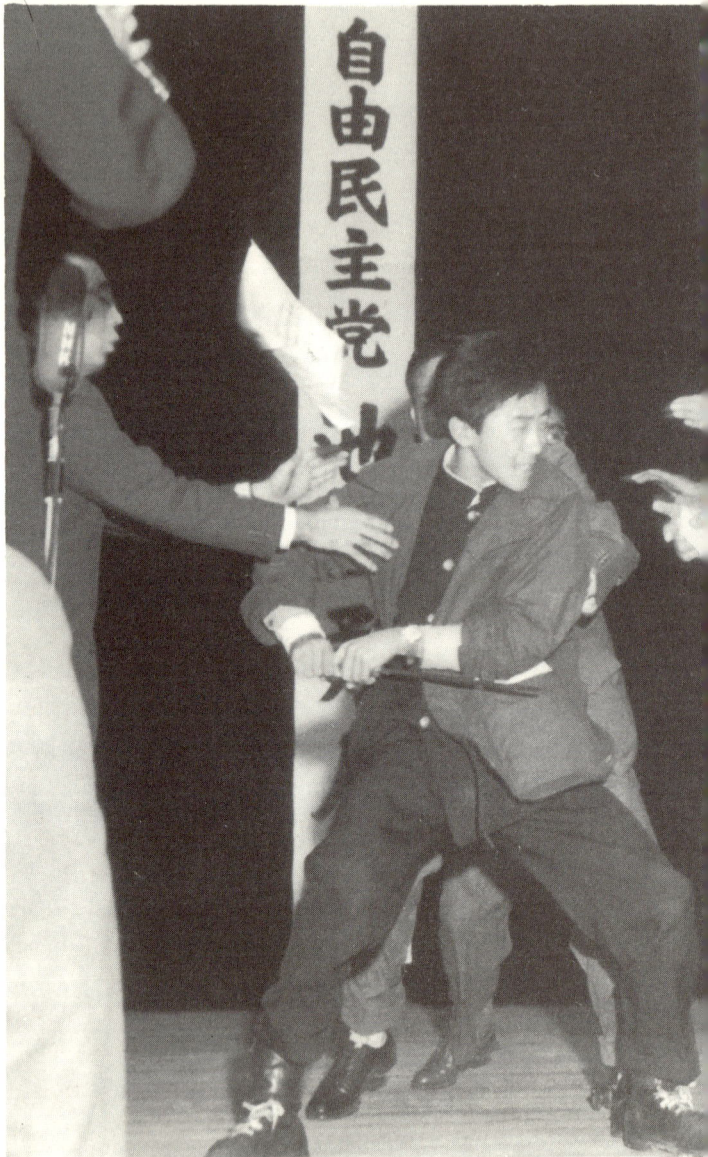

民主社会党 西尾末広氏

1960年（昭和35年）。政府の進める新
日米安保条約に反対の論陣を張ってい
た社会党委員長浅沼稲次郎は、この年
の10月12日に右翼青年に刺殺される。
憲法第51条では、「両議院の議員は、
議院で行つた演説、討論又は表決につ
いて、院外で責任を問はれない」とし
ているのだが……。
──写真・毎日新聞社

1960 Asanuma Inejirō, Chairman
of the Japan Socialist Party, led
the protest against the renewal
of the US-Japan Security Treaty.
He was stabbed to death by a
young right-wing activist on 12
October. Article 51 of the Constitution declares "members of both
Houses shall not be held liable
outside the House for speeches,
debates or votes cast inside the
House."

③前項但書の緊急集会において採られた措置は、臨時のものであつて、次の国会開会の後10日以内に、衆議院の同意がない場合には、その効力を失ふ。

第55条

両議院は、各〻その議員の資格に関する争訟を裁判する。但し、議員の議席を失はせるには、出席議員の3分の2以上の多数による議決を必要とする。

第56条

両議院は、各〻その総議員の3分の1以上の出席がなければ、議事を開き議決することができない。

②両議院の議事は、この憲法に特別の定のある場合を除いては、出席議員の過半数でこれを決し、可否同数のときは、議長の決するところによる。

第57条

両議院の会議は、公開とする。但し、出席議員の3分の2以上の多数で議決したときは、秘密会を開くことができる。

(3) Measures taken at such session as mentioned in the proviso of the preceding paragraph shall be provisional and shall become null and void unless agreed to by the House of Representatives within a period of ten (10) days after the opening of the next session of the Diet.

Article 55

Each House shall judge disputes related to qualifications of its members. However, in order to deny a seat to any member, it is necessary to pass a resolution by a majority of two-thirds or more of the members present.

Article 56

Business cannot be transacted in either House unless one-third or more of total membership is present.

(2) All matters shall be decided, in each House, by a majority of those present, except as elsewhere provided in the Constitution, and in case of a tie, the presiding officer shall decide the issue.

Article 57

Deliberation in each House shall be public. However, a secret meeting may be held where a majority of two-thirds or more of those members present passes a resolution therefor.

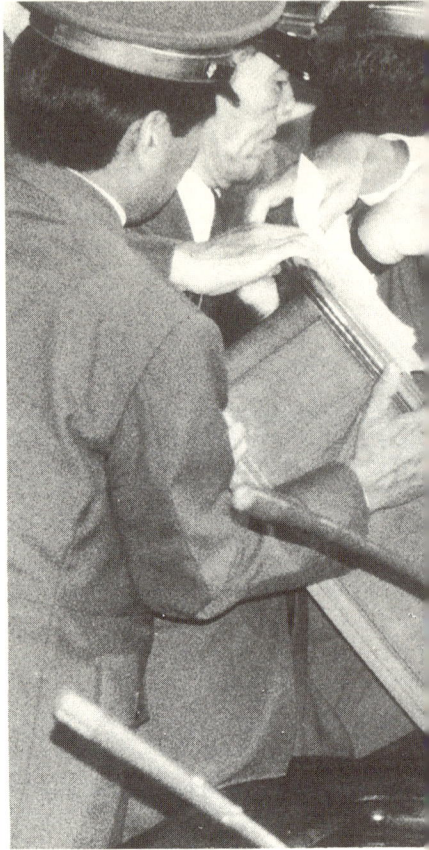

1992年（平成4年）。PKO国会で、社民連の菅直人は、時間をオーバーし
て論陣を張る。ルール違反ということで、衛視が壇上から引きずり降ろし
にかかる。その一方では、国会内の牛歩や座り込み戦術は容認されている。
庶民には熱弁の方が正常に映るのだが……。
　　　　　　　　　　　　　　　　　　　　　　——写真・朝日新聞社

1992 During Diet debate on Japan's role in peace-keeping operations overseas, Kan Naoto of the United Socialist Democratic
Party did not end his speech within his allotted time. Guards
were ordered to drag him from the podium. Other lawmakers
staged sit-ins and held up voting by literally taking hours to walk
to the front of the Diet to cast their ballots. The people wondered
what had happened to constructive debate.

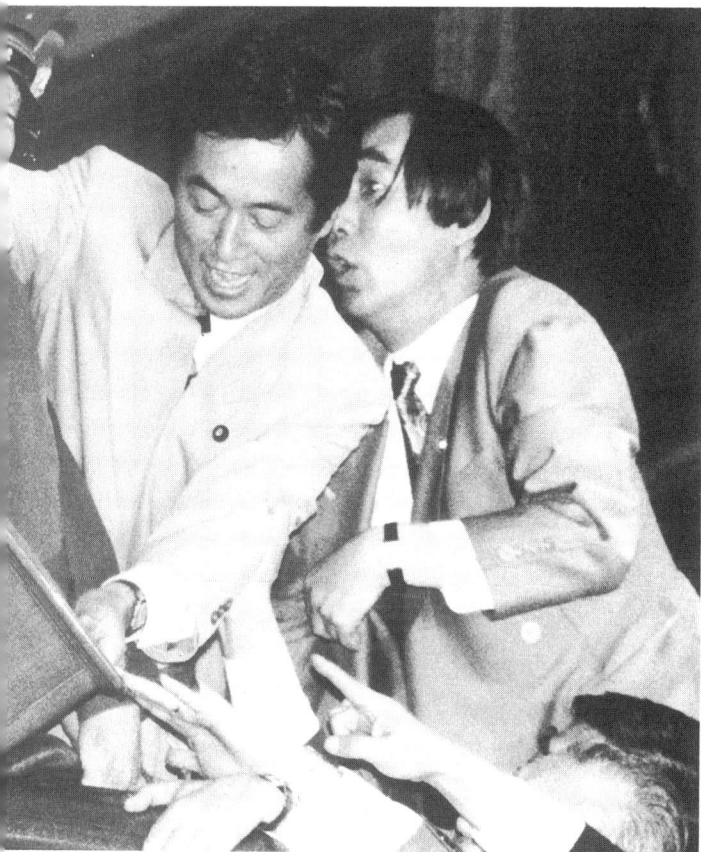

頒　布：広く配り分け
ること。配布。

②両議院は、各〻その会議の記録を保存し、秘密会の記録の中で特に秘密を要すると認められるもの以外は、これを公表し、且つ一般に頒布しなければならない。

③出席議員の5分の1以上の要求があれば、各議員の表決は、これを会議録に記載しなければならない。

第58条

両議院は、各〻その議長その他の役員を選任する。

②両議院は、各〻その会議その他の手続及び内部の規律に関する規則を定め、又、院内の秩序をみだした議員を懲罰することができる。但し、議員を除名するには、出席議員の3分の2以上の多数による議決を必要とする。

懲　罰：①不正・不当
な行いなどをこらしめ
罰すること。②国会や
地方議会で、秩序を乱
した議員を議決に基づ
いて処罰すること。戒
告、陳謝、登院・出席
停止、除名の4段階が
ある。

第59条

法律案は、この憲法に特別の定のある場合を除いては、両議院で可決したとき法律となる。

②衆議院で可決し、参議院でこれと異なつた議決をした法律案は、衆議院で出席議員の3分の2以上の多数で再び可決したときは、法律となる。

(2) Each House shall keep a record of proceedings. This record shall be published and given general circulation, excepting such parts of proceedings of secret session as may be deemed to require secrecy.

(3) Upon demand of one-fifth or more of the members present, votes of the members on any matter shall be recorded in the minutes.

Article 58

Each House shall select its own president and other officials.

(2) Each House shall establish its rules pertaining to meetings, proceedings and internal discipline, and may punish members for disorderly conduct. However, in order to expel a member, a majority of two-thirds or more of those members present must pass a resolution thereon.

Article 59

A bill becomes a law on passage by both Houses, except as otherwise provided by the Constitution.

(2) A bill which is passed by the House of Representatives, and upon which the House of Councillors makes a decision different from that of the House of Representatives, becomes a law when passed a second time by the House of Representatives by a majority of two-thirds or more of the members present.

1996年（平成8年）。「内閣総理大臣、橋本龍太郎さん」。議会の慣例
としての「君」づけを「さん」づけに変えたのは、女性で初の衆議
院議長に選出された土井たか子。だが、1996年秋の総選挙で社会党
党首に復帰し、彼女が議長職から退くと、国会は、「君」で呼ぶ世界
に戻った。

1996 Doi Takako, the first woman Speaker of the House of
Representatives, announced the prime minister as "Prime
Minister Hashimoto Ryūtarō-*san.*" Before Doi ascended to
the position of Speaker, lawmakers were addressed as *kun.*
Kun, as used in daily Japanese, refers only to men. After the
general election in the fall of 1996, Doi left her post to
become the chairperson of the Japan Socialist Party and
lawmakers went back to using *kun.*

③前項の規定は、法律の定めるところにより、衆議院が、両議院の協議会を開くことを求めることを妨げない。

④参議院が、衆議院の可決した法律案を受け取つた後、国会休会中の期間を除いて60日以内に、議決しないときは、衆議院は、参議院がその法律案を否決したものとみなすことができる。

第60条

予算は、さきに衆議院に提出しなければならない。

②予算について、参議院で衆議院と異なつた議決をした場合に、法律の定めるところにより、両議院の協議会を開いても意見が一致しないとき、又は参議院が、衆議院の可決した予算を受け取つた後、国会休会中の期間を除いて30日以内に、議決しないときは、衆議院の議決を国会の議決とする。

第61条

条約の締結に必要な国会の承認については、前条第2項の規定を準用する。

(3) The provision of the preceding paragraph does not preclude the House of Represenatatives from calling for the meeting of a joint committee of both Houses, provided for by law.

(4) Failure by the House of Councillors to take final action within sixty (60) days after receipt of a bill passed by the House of Representatives, time in recess excepted, may be determined by the House of Representatives to constitute a rejection of the said bill by the House of Councillors.

Article 60

The budget must first be submitted to the House of Representatives.

(2) Upon consideration of the budget, when the House of Councillors makes a decision different from that of the House of Representatives, and when no agreement can be reached even through a joint committee of both Houses, provided for by law, or in the case of failure by the House of Councillors to take final action within thirty (30) days, the period of recess excluded, after the receipt of the budget passed by the House of Representatives, the decision of the House of Representatives shall be the decision of the Diet.

Article 61

The second paragraph of the preceding article applies also to the Diet approval required for the conclusion of treaties.

1946年（昭和21年）。最後の帝国議会が女性の最初の舞台となった。日本国憲法の公布を待たずに、女性参政権を認めた新選挙法のもと、39人の婦人代議士が誕生。彼女達も新憲法を議論した。

1946 The last Imperial Diet meeting was the first platform for women after they were granted the right to vote and run for office in 1945. Although the new Constitution had not yet been enacted, under the New Election Law, 39 women were elected to the House of Representatives where they discussed the new Constitution.

第62条

両議院は、各〻国政に関する調査を行ひ、これに関して、証人の出頭及び証言並びに記録の提出を要求することができる。

第63条

内閣総理大臣その他の国務大臣は、両議院の一に議席を有すると有しないとにかかはらず、何時でも議案について発言するため議院に出席することができる。又、答弁又は説明のため出席を求められたときは、出席しなければならない。

第64条

国会は、罷免の訴追を受けた裁判官を裁判するため、両議院の議員で組織する弾劾裁判所を設ける。

②弾劾に関する事項は、法律でこれを定める。

訴　追：①検察官が刑事事件について公訴を起こすこと。②裁判官や人事官などの弾劾の申し立てをし、罷免を求めること。

弾　劾：①罪を調べて責任を追及すること。②大統領・大臣・裁判官など、身分を保障された者の非行を議会が訴追し、これを罷免する手続き。日本では、裁判官だけが対象になる。

Article 62

Each House may conduct investigations in relation to government, and may demand the presence and testimony of witnesses, and the production of records.

Article 63

The Prime Minister and other Ministers of State may, at any time, appear in either House for the purpose of speaking on bills, regardless of whether they are members of the House or not. They must appear when their presence is required in order to give answers or explanations.

Article 64

The Diet shall set up an impeachment court from among the members of both Houses for the purpose of trying those judges against whom removal proceedings have been instituted.

(2) Matters relating to impeachment shall be provided by law.

1976年 (昭和51年)。「記憶にございません」。その年の流行語にもなっ
たこの言葉。総理大臣を巻き込んでの汚職疑惑となったロッキード事
件。衆議院予算委員会は、憲法第62条に基づき、疑惑のかかった国際
興業社主小佐野賢治を証人として喚問。これを契機に国会での証人喚
問が注目されるようになるが、一方では、証人の人権問題なども提起
され、テレビ中継が静止画像にされるなどして、今日に至っている。
　　　　　　　　　　　　　　　　　　　　　　　　──写真・PANA通信

1976 Article 62 of the Constitution gives the Diet the right to
demand the presence and testimony of witnesses. At the
time of the Lockheed scandal, involving bribes and kickbacks
to politicians, Osano Kenji was questioned by Diet members.
In response, he repeatedly said, "I have no recollection of that."
This phrase became widely used among the general public.
During the scandal, the rights of the witnesses became an
issue. Live television broadcasts of the testimony of witnesses were replaced with audio-only broadcasts.

| 第5章 | 内 閣 |

第65条
行政権(ぎょうせいけん)は、内閣に属する。

第66条
内閣は、法律の定めるところにより、その首長(しゅちょう)たる内閣総理大臣及びその他の国務大臣でこれを組織する。

②内閣総理大臣その他の国務大臣は、文民(ぶんみん)でなければならない。

③内閣は、行政権の行使について、国会に対し連帯して責任を負ふ。

第67条
内閣総理大臣は、国会議員の中から国会の議決で、これを指名する。この指名は、他のすべての案件(あんけん)に先だつて、これを行ふ。

②衆議院と参議院とが異なつた指名の議決をした場合に、法律の定めるところにより、両議院の協議会を開いても意見が一致しないとき、又は衆議院が指名の議決をした後、国会休会中の期間を除いて10日以内に、参議院が、指名の議決をしないときは、衆議院の議決を国会の議決とする。

国務大臣：内閣を構成する閣僚。狭義では総理大臣を除く。首相が任免権をもち、過半数は国会議員であることが必要。国務相。

文 民：職業軍人でない国民。

CHAPTER V   THE CABINET

Article 65

Executive power shall be vested in the Cabinet.

Article 66

The Cabinet shall consist of the Prime Minister, who shall be its head, and other Ministers of State, as provided for by law.

(2) The Prime Minister and other Ministers of State must be civilians.

(3) The Cabinet, in the exercise of executive power, shall be collectively responsible to the Diet.

Article 67

The Prime Minister shall be designated from among the members of the Diet by a resolution of the Diet. This designation shall precede all other business.

(2) If the House of Representatives and the House of Councillors disagree and if no agreement can be reached even through a joint committee of both Houses, provided for by law, or the House of Councillors fails to make designation within ten (10) days, exclusive of the period of recess, after the House of Representatives has made designation, the decision of the House of Representatives shall be the decision of the Diet.

1974年（昭和49年）。日本列島改造論をひっさげ、1972年に首班指名を受けた田中角栄首相。しかし、政治資金スキャンダルを世論から追及され、1974年11月、この疑惑釈明会見直後に退陣した。
——写真・毎日新聞社

1974 Tanaka Kakuei was chosen as Japan's prime minister in 1972, under promises to reform the country. Despite an attempt at vindicating himself in a press conference, public anger over a political funds scandal forced him to step down in November 1974.

第68条

　内閣総理大臣は、国務大臣を任命する。但し、その過半数は、国会議員の中から選ばれなければならない。

　②内閣総理大臣は、任意に国務大臣を罷免することができる。

第69条

　内閣は、衆議院で不信任の決議案を可決し、又は信任の決議案を否決したときは、10日以内に衆議院が解散されない限り、総辞職をしなければならない。

第70条

　内閣総理大臣が欠けたとき、又は衆議院議員総選挙の後に初めて国会の召集があつたときは、内閣は、総辞職をしなければならない。

第71条

　前2条の場合には、内閣は、あらたに内閣総理大臣が任命されるまで引き続きその職務を行ふ。

第72条

　内閣総理大臣は、内閣を代表して議案を国会に提出し、一般国務及び外交関係について国会に報告し、並びに行政各部を指揮監督する。

Article 68

The Prime Minister shall appoint the Ministers of State. However, a majority of their number must be chosen from among the members of the Diet.

(2) The Prime Minister may remove the Ministers of State as he chooses.

Article 69

If the House of Representatives passes a non-confidence resolution, or rejects a confidence resolution, the Cabinet shall resign en masse, unless the House of Representatives is dissolved within ten (10) days.

Article 70

When there is a vacancy in the post of Prime Minister, or upon the first convocation of the Diet after a general election of members of the House of Representatives, the Cabinet shall resign en masse.

Article 71

In the cases mentioned in the two preceding articles, the Cabinet shall continue its functions until the time when a new Prime Minister is appointed.

Article 72

The Prime Minister, representing the Cabinet, submits bills, reports on general national affairs and foreign relations to the Diet and exercises control and supervision over various administrative branches.

102

1954年（昭和29年）。造船業界からのヤミ献金捜査
で、検察当局は与党自由党幹事長佐藤栄作の逮捕
を決定。だが、時の法務大臣犬養健は、逮捕の許
諾請求は承認できない旨、検事総長に通知。犬養
は、憲法第72条により「行政各部を指揮監督する」
権限を持つ内閣総理大臣の吉田茂に、この指揮権
発動を強く促されたと言われている。犬養は、翌
日辞職する。これにより、佐藤栄作は検察の追及
を免れ、事件は闇に葬られた。

—写真・共同通信社

1954 When Satō Eisaku, Secretary General
of the ruling Liberal Party, was indicted for
accepting bribes from shipbuilding compa-
nies, Inukai Takeru, Minister of Justice, sent
a note to the Public Prosecutor General,
refusing to approve prosecution. It is believed
that Inukai exercised his authority under
pressure from Prime Minister Yoshida
Shigeru, who under Article 72 of the Constitution has the authority to control and
supervise various administrative branches.
Inukai resigned the next day. The scandal
seemed to just fade away.

104

第73条

内閣は、他の一般行政事務の外、左の事務を行ふ。

1　法律を誠実に執行し、国務を総理すること。

2　外交関係を処理すること。

3　条約を締結すること。但し、事前に、時宜によつては事後に、国会の承認を経ることを必要とする。

4　法律の定める基準に従ひ、官吏に関する事務を掌理すること。

5　予算を作成して国会に提出すること。

6　この憲法及び法律の規定を実施するために、政令を制定すること。但し、政令には、特にその法律の委任がある場合を除いては、罰則を設けることができない。

7　大赦、特赦、減刑、刑の執行の免除及び復権を決定すること。

第74条

法律及び政令には、すべて主任の国務大臣が署名し、内閣総理大臣が連署することを必要とする。

官　吏：国家公務員。官員。

掌　理：しっかり取り扱って、処理すること。管理し、取りまとめること。

政　令：内閣が制定する命令。効力は法律に劣り、省令や府令にまさる。法律の委任がなければ罰則を設けたり、義務を課することはできない。

Article 73

The Cabinet, in addition to other general administrative functions, shall perform the following functions:

(i) Administer the law faithfully; conduct affairs of state;

(ii) Manage foreign affairs;

(iii) Conclude treaties. However, it shall obtain prior or, depending on circumstances, subsequent approval of the Diet;

(iv) Administer the civil service, in accordance with standards established by law;

(v) Prepare the budget, and present it to the Diet;

(vi) Enact cabinet orders in order to execute the provisions of this Constitution and of the law. However, it cannot include penal provisions in such cabinet orders unless authorized by such law.

(vii) Decide on general amnesty, special amnesty, commutation of punishment, reprieve, and restoration of rights.

Article 74

All laws and cabinet orders shall be signed by the competent Minister of State and countersigned by the Prime Minister.

THE PRIME MINISTE

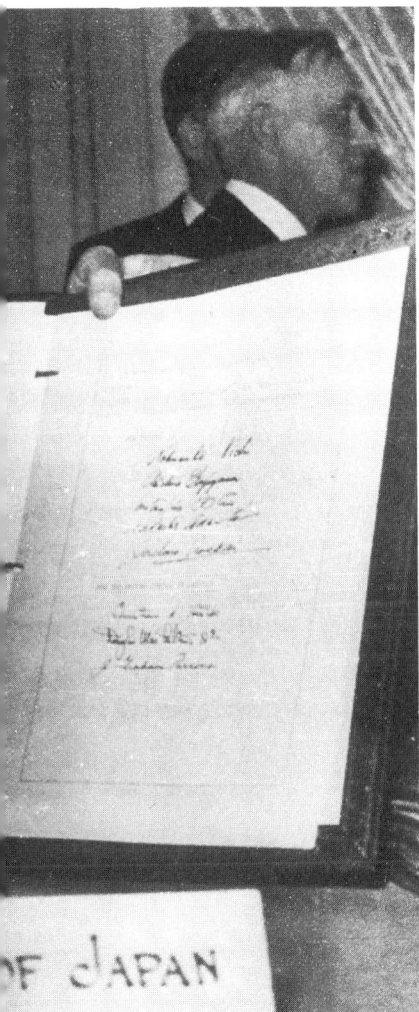

OF JAPAN

1960年（昭和35年）。新日米安保条約の調印を終え、条約文書を示す岸信介首相。憲法第73条により、自らが先頭に立ち、内閣の権限でアメリカとの条約締結をリード。だが国会での承認に際しては、野党と世論の強い反対にあい、足踏みを強いられた。

──写真・PANA通信

1960 Prime Minister Kishi Nobusuke displays the revised US-Japan Security Treaty after the signing ceremony. He negotiated the treaty with the United States under the authority given to the cabinet by Article 73 of the Constitution. But when it came time for Diet approval, he had to contend with public protests and resistance from opposition parties.

第75条

　国務大臣は、その在任中、内閣総理大臣の同意がなければ、訴追されない。但し、これがため、訴追の権利は、害されない。

Article 75

The Ministers of State, during their tenure of office, shall not be subject to legal action without the consent of the Prime Minister. However, the right to take that action is not impaired hereby.

1971年（昭和46年）。6月17日に沖縄返還協定（「琉球諸島及び大東諸島に関する日本国とアメリカ合衆国との間の協定」）が調印された。愛知揆一外相とロジャーズ国務長官が同時に署名。沖縄は、1972年5月15日に日本に返還された。

1971 Aichi Kiichi, Minister for Foreign Affairs, signs the agreement between Japan and the United States concerning the Ryūkyū Islands and the Daitō Islands. Okinawa was reunited with Japan on 15 May 1972.

第6章　司 法

第76条

　すべて司法権は、最高裁判所及び法律の定めるところにより設置する下級裁判所に属する。

　②特別裁判所は、これを設置することができない。行政機関は、終審として裁判を行ふことができない。

　③すべて裁判官は、その良心に従ひ独立してその職権を行ひ、この憲法及び法律にのみ拘束される。

第77条

　最高裁判所は、訴訟に関する手続、弁護士、裁判所の内部規律及び司法事務処理に関する事項について、規則を定める権限を有する。

　②検察官は、最高裁判所の定める規則に従はなければならない。

　③最高裁判所は、下級裁判所に関する規則を定める権限を、下級裁判所に委任することができる。

特別裁判所：特殊な事件や人を対象とする裁判所。旧制下の行政裁判所など。

Chapter VI JUDICIARY

Article 76

The whole judicial power is vested in a Supreme Court and in such inferior courts as are established by law.

(2) No extraordinary tribunal shall be established, nor shall any organ or agency of the Executive be given final judicial power.

(3) All judges shall be independent in the exercise of their conscience and shall be bound only by this Constitution and the laws.

Article 77

The Supreme Court is vested with the rule-making power under which it determines the rules of procedure and of practice, and of matters relating to attorneys, the internal discipline of the courts and the administration of judicial affairs.

(2) Public procurators shall be subject to the rule-making power of the Supreme Court.

(3) The Supreme Court may delegate the power to make rules for inferior courts to such courts.

1947年（昭和22年）。ヤミ米摘発が自分の仕事ということで、自らは
一切ヤミ米を買わずに栄養失調死した山口良忠判事。「すべて裁判官
は、その良心に従ひ独立してその職権を行ひ、この憲法及び法律に
のみ拘束される」という憲法第76条の一文に殉じたわけだが、「国民
生活の実状にそぐわない食管法を放置する国家への抗議の死」と評
する声もあった。　　──記事・『朝日新聞』1947年11月5日号より

1947 Yamaguchi Yoshitada, a court judge, took it on himself
to prosecute traders in black market rice. Refusing to eat
even a single grain of black market rice, he chose to starve
himself to death. He was following Article 76 of the Constitution that states "judges shall be independent in the exercise of their conscience and be bound by only by this
Constitution and the laws." Some said his death was in
protest of the Stable Food Control Law, a law that failed to
reflect reality.

判事がヤミを拒み
榮養失調で死亡

遺した日誌で明るみへ

山口良忠判事

安い給料で食えぬ、闇米事をひく弁護士に編纂してゆく折柄、いまこそ判検事は法の威信に殉じなければならないとギリギリの瀬戸から、一切のヤミを拒否して困苦生活をまもりつづけ、随意の栄養失調でたおれた若き検事の話が、このほど下に明るみに出た。

良忠ちゃん、やっ……と、二歳になられる、十六号棟の判事、月に三千円（税込）足らずでは、押しなべて妻子ある同胞はほとんど毎日止まるばかりするよりほかなく、配給もはけばかりであった……このような窮乏判床日記を残し……町の食糧に偽装といそしんだが、病床でヤミ食糧をしりぞいた歓びや愛されながら……

判事、弁護士も踏み入らぬ在京事、弁護士も踏み入らぬ在京事……

法を守り死の行進

[佐賀] 死の床につづられた日記の一節（原文のまま）

食事統制法は悪法だ、しかし法律である以上、國民は絶対にこれに服従せねばならない自分だけが自分の目の生活は全く死の行進だそれでもヤミ買に出ることは苦しくともヤミ質……にもひそかにヤミ買で何ら知ぬ間で役所に出ているのに、自分は今やっとして消い死の行進を続けていることを思うと……増した専心審理の勤労の幾案です

[各段落] 山口判事の日記

第78条

　裁判官は、裁判により、心身の故障のために職務を執ることができないと決定された場合を除いては、公の弾劾によらなければ罷免されない。裁判官の懲戒処分は、行政機関がこれを行ふことはできない。

第79条

　最高裁判所は、その長たる裁判官及び法律の定める員数のその他の裁判官でこれを構成し、その長たる裁判官以外の裁判官は、内閣でこれを任命する。

　②最高裁判所の裁判官の任命は、その任命後初めて行はれる衆議院議員総選挙の際国民の審査に付し、その後10年を経過した後初めて行はれる衆議院議員総選挙の際更に審査に付し、その後も同様とする。

　③前項の場合において、投票者の多数が裁判官の罷免を可とするときは、その裁判官は、罷免される。

　④審査に関する事項は、法律でこれを定める。

　⑤最高裁判所の裁判官は、法律の定める年齢に達した時に退官する。

　⑥最高裁判所の裁判官は、すべて定期に相当額の報酬を受ける。この報酬は、在任中、これを減額することができない。

Article 78

Judges shall not be removed except by public impeachment unless judicially declared mentally or physically incompetent to perform official duties. No disciplinary action against judges shall be administered by any executive organ or agency.

Article 79

The Supreme Court shall consist of a Chief Judge and such number of judges as may be determined by law; all such judges excepting the Chief Judge shall be appointed by the Cabinet.

(2) The appointment of the judges of the Supreme Court shall be reviewed by the people at the first general election of members of the House of Representatives following their appointment, and shall be reviewed again at the first general election of members of the House of Representatives after a lapse of ten (10) years, and in the same manner thereafter.

(3) In cases mentioned in the foregoing paragraph, when the majority of the voters favors the dismissal of a judge, he shall be dismissed.

(4) Matters pertaining to review shall be prescribed by law.

(5) The judges of the Supreme Court shall be retired upon the attainment of the age as fixed by law.

(6) All such judges shall receive, at regular stated intervals, adequate compensation which shall not be decreased during their terms of office.

立法、行政、司法と三権分立の原則にたつ日本国憲法によって、司法の頂点に立つだけでなく、違憲審査権を持つ。憲法第81条は「最高裁判所は、一切の法律、命令、規則又は処分が憲法に適合するかしないかを決定する権限を有する終審裁判所である」と定めている。

The Supreme Court Article 81 of the Constitution states that the "Supreme Court is the court of last resort with power to determine the constitutionality of any law, order, regulation or official act."

第80条

下級裁判所の裁判官は、最高裁判所の指名した者の名簿によつて、内閣でこれを任命する。その裁判官は、任期を10年とし、再任されることができる。但し、法律の定める年齢に達した時には退官する。

②下級裁判所の裁判官は、すべて定期に相当額の報酬を受ける。この報酬は、在任中、これを減額することができない。

第81条

最高裁判所は、一切(いつさい)の法律、命令、規則又は処分が憲法に適合するかしないかを決定する権限を有する終審裁判所である。

第82条

裁判の対審(たいしん)及び判決は、公開法廷でこれを行ふ。

②裁判所が、裁判官の全員一致で、公の秩序又は善良の風俗を害する虞(おそれ)があると決した場合には、対審は、公開しないでこれを行ふことができる。但し、政治犯罪、出版に関する犯罪又はこの憲法第3章で保障する国民の権利が問題となつてゐる事件の対審は、常(つね)にこれを公開しなければならない。

対　審：訴訟手続きにおいて、原告と被告を法廷で立ち会わせて主張や立証の機会を与え審理すること。民事訴訟では口頭弁論、刑事訴訟では公判手続きをさす。

Article 80

The judges of the inferior courts shall be appointed by the Cabinet from a list of persons nominated by the Supreme Court. All such judges shall hold office for a term of ten (10) years with privilege of reappointment, provided that they shall be retired upon the attainment of the age as fixed by law.

(2) The judges of the inferior courts shall receive, at regular stated intervals, adequate compensation which shall not be decreased during their terms of office.

Article 81

The Supreme Court is the court of last resort with power to determine the constitutionality of any law, order, regulation or official act.

Article 82

Trials shall be conducted and judgment declared publicly.

(2) Where a court unanimously determines publicity to be dangerous to public order or morals, a trial may be conducted privately, but trials of political offenses, offenses involving the press or cases wherein the rights of people as guaranteed in Chapter III of this Constitution are in question shall always be conducted publicly.

1996年（平成 8 年）。憲法第82条の規定に則り、裁判は公開で進められる。ただし、開かれた法廷ではあるが、写真やテレビによる撮影は原則として認められていない。このため、オウム真理教の前教団代表松本（麻原）被告の裁判など、国民の関心を集める裁判の際は、新聞、テレビなどのマスコミは、スケッチ要員を配して取材と報道にあたっている。　　　　　　　　　──イラスト構成・大須賀友一／毎日新聞社

1996 Article 82 of the Constitution instructs that trials must be conducted publicly. While seating capacity is the only constraint on public access, no cameras are allowed. At trials that draw wide public interest, such as the one of Aum Shinrikyō cult leader Asahara Shōkō, newspapers, television and other media rely on sketches to portray the proceedings.

第7章　財　政

第83条

　国の財政を処理する権限は、国会の議決に基いて、これを行使しなければならない。

第84条

　あらたに租税を課し、又は現行の租税を変更するには、法律又は法律の定める条件によることを必要とする。

第85条

　国費を支出し、又は国が債務を負担するには、国会の議決に基くことを必要とする。

第86条

　内閣は、毎会計年度の予算を作成し、国会に提出して、その審議を受け議決を経なければならない。

第87条

　予見し難い予算の不足に充てるため、国会の議決に基いて予備費を設け、内閣の責任でこれを支出することができる。

　②すべて予備費の支出については、内閣は、事後に国会の承諾を得なければならない。

租　税：①租と税。田租とその他の庸・調など。上納するものとされたもの。年貢。②国家・地方公共団体が経費にあてるため、国民・住民から強制的にとりたてる金銭。国税と地方税。税金。税。

Chapter VII FINANCE

Article 83

The power to administer national finances shall be exercised as the Diet shall determine.

Article 84

No new taxes shall be imposed or existing ones modified except by law or under such conditions as law may prescribe.

Article 85

No money shall be expended, nor shall the State obligate itself, except as authorized by the Diet.

Article 86

The Cabinet shall prepare and submit to the Diet for its consideration and decision a budget for each fiscal year.

Article 87

In order to provide for unforeseen deficiencies in the budget, a reserve fund may be authorized by the Diet to be expended upon the responsibility of the Cabinet.

(2) The Cabinet must get subsequent approval of the Diet for all payments from the reserve fund.

1995年（平成7年）。1月17日に阪神・淡路地域を襲った阪神大震災は、6,400人を越える命を奪い、被災地は今も再建途上にある。ところが、「公共事業へは支出できるが個人へは支給できない」という国の財政システムに、異論続出。　　——写真・池田栄次

1995 On 17 January, the Kōbe area was hit by the devastating Great Hanshin Earthquake that took more than 6,400 lives. The destroyed area has still not been completely rebuilt. People protested that the government's financial system provides money for public businesses but not for individual victims' rebuilding.

第88条

　すべて皇室財産は、国に属する。すべて皇室
の費用は、予算に計上して国会の議決を経なけ
ればならない。

第89条

　公金その他の公の財産は、宗教上の組織若し
くは団体の使用、便益若しくは維持のため、又
は公の支配に属しない慈善、教育若しくは博愛
の事業に対し、これを支出し、又はその利用に
供してはならない。

第90条

　国の収入支出の決算は、すべて毎年会計検査
院がこれを検査し、内閣は、次の年度に、その
検査報告とともに、これを国会に提出しなけれ
ばならない。

　②会計検査院の組織及び権限は、法律でこれ
を定める。

第91条

　内閣は、国会及び国民に対し、定期に、少く
とも毎年1回、国の財政状況について報告しな
ければならない。

Article 88

All property of the Imperial Household shall belong to the State. All expenses of the Imperial Household shall be appropriated by the Diet in the budget.

Article 89

No public money or other property shall be expended or appropriated for the use, benefit or maintenance of any religious institution or association, or for any charitable, educational or benevolent enterprises not under the control of public authority.

Article 90

Final accounts of the expenditures and revenues of the State shall be audited annually by a Board of Audit and submitted by the Cabinet to the Diet, together with the statement of audit, during the fiscal year immediately following the period covered.

(2) The organization and competency of the Board of Audit shall be determined by law.

Article 91

At regular intervals and at least annually the Cabinet shall report to the Diet and the people on the state of national finances.

「玉ぐし

靖国神社への
愛媛県の支出　宗

愛媛玉ぐし料訴訟判決で最高裁に入る原告・弁護団＝2日午後2時15分、東京都千代田区事町で

特措法改正

「政府案賛

小沢氏　首相

橋本龍太郎首相（自民党総裁）と新進党の小沢一郎党首は、二日夜、沖縄の米軍用地の強制使用継続の問題をめぐって、首相官邸で会談した。橋本首相は日米安保条約上の義務を果たす必要があるとの立場から駐留軍用地特別措置法（特措法）を改正して対応する考え

1997年（平成９年）。玉串料に違憲判決。日本国憲法第20条や第89条などでは、政治と宗教の分離をうたっている。これは、国家神道が全体主義の道具になったという負の歴史の反省にたっている。この判決は、首相や閣僚の靖国神社への公式参拝などをめぐる議論などにも影響を及ぼすのかも知れない。
——記事・『朝日新聞』４月３日号より

1997 Articles 20 and 89 of the Constitution ensure the separation of religion and state. This is a reflection on the role played by State Shintō in encouraging nationalism during the war. The Supreme Court has now ruled that even nominal donations from public funds to Shintō shrines are unconstitutional. This may affect the debate on "official visits" by government employees to Yasukuni Shrine.

「公費」違憲判決

的活動と最高裁

朝日新聞

発行所 東京都中央区築地５丁目
３番２号郵便番号１０４-１１
電話０３-３５４５-０１３１
朝日新聞東京本社
郵便振替口座 ００１００-７-１７３０
©朝日新聞東京本社 1997

参拝論議にも影響

愛媛県が靖国神社に納めた玉ぐし料など遺公費で負担したのは政教分離を定めた憲法に違反するとして、住民が当時の県知事らを相手取り、支出した金を県に賠償するよう求めた「愛媛玉ぐし料訴訟」上告審で、最高裁大法廷（裁判長・三好達長官）は二日、「公費支出は憲法が禁止した宗教的活動に当たる」という初めての判断を示した。そのうえで、合憲判断に立って請求を退けた二審判決を破棄し、改めて十六万八千円の支払いを前知事に命じる逆転判決を言い渡した。

（32面に判決理由要旨、2・3・33・34・35面に関係記事）

前知事に賠償命じる

審理では、三月に退官した可部恒雄裁判官を含む十五人の全裁判官が関与した。論理構成には違いがあるものの、このうち十三人が違憲と判断。三好長官と可部裁判官が合憲とする反対意見を明らかにした。

判決は、これまで玉ぐし料などの公費支出を見送ってきた自治体に対し、将来にわたって歯止めをかけるだけでなく、首相や閣僚による公式参拝論議など「靖国」をめぐる国の対応にも影響を及ぼすものとみられる。

●愛媛県による玉ぐし料などの公費支出は、憲法二〇条三項が禁止する宗教的活動に当たる。

●目的効果基準を踏襲
多数意見は政教分離原則について、国家が宗教とかかわりを持つことを全く許さないとするものではない

子
●愛媛県による玉ぐし料などの公費的支出は、憲法二〇条三項が禁止する宗教的活動に当たる。

| 第8章 | 地方自治 |

第92条

　地方公共団体の組織及び運営に関する事項
は、地方自治の本旨に基いて、法律でこれを定
める。

第93条

　地方公共団体には、法律の定めるところによ
り、その議事機関として議会を設置する。

　②地方公共団体の長、その議会の議員及び法
律の定めるその他の吏員は、その地方公共団体
の住民が、直接これを選挙する。

第94条

　地方公共団体は、その財産を管理し、事務を
処理し、及び行政を執行する権能を有し、法律
の範囲内で条例を制定することができる。

第95条

　一の地方公共団体のみに適用される特別法
は、法律の定めるところにより、その地方公共
団体の住民の投票においてその過半数の同意を
得なければ、国会は、これを制定することがで
きない。

Chapter VIII LOCAL SELF-GOVERNMENT

Article 92

Regulations concerning organization and operations of local public entities shall be fixed by law in accordance with the principle of local autonomy.

Article 93

The local public entities shall establish assemblies as their deliberative organs, in accordance with law.

(2) The chief executive officers of all local public entities, the members of their assemblies, and such other local officials as may be determined by law shall be elected by direct popular vote within their several communities.

Article 94

Local public entities shall have the right to manage their property, affairs and administration and to enact their own regulations within law.

Article 95

A special law, applicable only to one local public entity, cannot be enacted by the Diet without the consent of the majority of the voters of the local public entity concerned, obtained in accordance with law.

1989年（平成元年）。「ふるさと創生」をかかげた竹下登内閣は、全国の自治体に使途を指定しないで１億円ずつを配布。中には金塊にして住民に見せる自治体も。憲法による地方自治の理念と、地方の統治力の現実とのギャップを巡って様々な意見が出された。　　　　　　　　　　　──写真・読売ニュース写真

1989 When Takeshita Noboru became prime minister, he promised to help areas outside of the main cities. He distributed 100 million yen to each local government entity. One city used the money to buy gold. His policies created debate about the constitutional rights of local governments.

第9章　改 正

第96条

　この憲法の改正は、各議院の総議員の3分の
2以上の賛成で、国会が、これを発議し、国民
に提案してその承認を経なければならない。こ
の承認には、特別の国民投票又は国会の定める
選挙の際行はれる投票において、その過半数の
賛成を必要とする。

　②憲法改正について前項の承認を経たとき
は、天皇は、国民の名で、この憲法と一体を成
すものとして、直ちにこれを公布する。

Chapter IX AMENDMENTS

Article 96

Amendments to this Constitution shall be initiated by the Diet, through a concurring vote of two-thirds or more of all the members of each House and shall thereupon be submitted to the people for ratification, which shall require the affirmative vote of a majority of all votes cast thereon, at a special referendum or at such election as the Diet shall specify.

(2) Amendments when so ratified shall immediately be promulgated by the Emperor in the name of the people, as an integral part of this Constitution.

1992年（平成3年）。改憲か護憲か、憲法が誕生以来絶え間なく続くこの議論。かつて改憲と言えば憲法の否定という色彩が強かった。しかし冷戦の終結と国際関係のさらなるグローバル化は、これまでとは違った構図を作り出した。PKOに関しては、憲法前文にある国際協調主義を尊重するからこそ、国連の平和活動のために自衛隊を派遣するのだという論議になった。（写真はペルシャ湾に向かうPKOの掃海艇派遣部隊）

1992 Ever since the Constitution was enacted, its revision has been debated. Some have thought that any modifications or revisions would destroy it. But with the end of the cold war, Japan is becoming more global and opinions are changing. The PKO maneuvers were debated on the basis that the Preamble of the Constitution urges respect for international cooperation, and that dispatch of the Self Defence Forces would be for the United Nations' peacekeeping purposes.

第10章 最高法規

第97条

　この憲法が日本国民に保障する基本的人権は、人類の多年にわたる自由獲得の努力の成果であつて、これらの権利は、過去幾多の試錬に堪へ、現在及び将来の国民に対し、侵すことのできない永久の権利として信託されたものである。

第98条

　この憲法は、国の最高法規であつて、その条規に反する法律、命令、詔勅及び国務に関するその他の行為の全部又は一部は、その効力を有しない。

　②日本国が締結した条約及び確立された国際法規は、これを誠実に遵守することを必要とする。

第99条

　天皇又は摂政及び国務大臣、国会議員、裁判官その他の公務員は、この憲法を尊重し擁護する義務を負ふ。

Chapter X SUPREME LAW

Article 97

The fundamental human rights by this Constitution guaranteed to the people of Japan are fruits of the age-old struggle of man to be free; they have survived the many exacting tests for durability and are conferred upon this and future generations in trust, to be held for all time inviolate.

Article 98

This Constitution shall be the supreme law of the nation and no law, ordinance, imperial rescript or other act of government, or part thereof, contrary to the provisions hereof, shall have legal force or validity.

(2) The treaties concluded by Japan and established laws of nations shall be faithfully observed.

Article 99

The Emperor or the Regent as well as Ministers of State, members of the Diet, judges, and all other public officials have the obligation to respect and uphold this Constitution.

1970年（昭和45年）。日本国憲法は一切の軍事力を否定している。だが、日米安保条約にともなう米軍の駐留は、憲法で保障された豊かで平穏な生活の上を、今日もかすめてゆく。

———写真・栗原達男

1970 Under the Constitution, Japan is not allowed to maintain military forces of any kind. But in accordance with the US-Japan Security Treaty, American troops are kept in Japan. Fighter aircraft flying overhead contrasts with the wholesome and peaceful way of Japanese life guaranteed by the Constitution.

第 11 章　補　則

施　行：①実地に行う
こと。実行。実施。②
《「せこう」とも》法令
が制定されたのち、そ
の効力を現実に発生さ
せること。法律は公布
の日から20日後に施
行されるのが原則。

第100条

　この憲法は、公布の日から起算して 6 箇月を経過した日から、これを施行する。

　②この憲法を施行するために必要な法律の制定、参議院議員の選挙及び国会召集の手続並びにこの憲法を施行するために必要な準備手続は、前項の期日よりも前に、これを行ふことができる。

第101条

　この憲法施行の際、参議院がまだ成立してゐないときは、その成立するまでの間、衆議院は、国会としての権限を行ふ。

第102条

　この憲法による第 1 期の参議院議員のうち、その半数の者の任期は、これを 3 年とする。その議員は、法律の定めるところにより、これを定める。

CHAPTER XI SUPPLEMENTARY PROVISIONS

Article 100

This Constitution shall be enforced as from the day when the period of six months will have elapsed counting from the day of its promulgation.

(2) The enactment of laws necessary for the enforcement of this Constitution, the election of members of the House of Councillors and the procedure for the convocation of the Diet and other preparatory procedures necessary for the enforcement of this Constitution may be executed before the day prescribed in the preceding paragraph.

Article 101

If the House of Councillors is not constituted before the effective date of this Constitution, the House of Representatives shall function as the Diet until such time as the House of Councillors shall be constituted.

Article 102

The term of office for half the members of the House of Councillors serving in the first term under this Constitution shall be three years. Members falling under this category shall be determined in accordance with law.

1958年（昭和33年）。わが家に車がやってきた。終戦直後は車の製造は禁止されていたが、この年、軽量廉価版乗用車スバル360が発売され大好評。この2年後の1960年、池田勇人首相は国民所得倍増計画を掲げ、日本列島は豊かさへの疾走を開始する。

1958 Production of automobiles was banned for a short time after the war. In 1958, the compact and inexpensive SUBARU 360 was a big hit. In 1960, Prime Minister Ikeda Hayato announced a plan to double Japan's household income. Japan began the race towards affluence.

第103条

　この憲法施行の際現に在職する国務大臣、衆議院議員及び裁判官並びにその他の公務員で、その地位に相応する地位がこの憲法で認められてゐる者は、法律で特別の定をした場合を除いては、この憲法施行のため、当然にはその地位を失ふことはない。但し、この憲法によつて、後任者が選挙又は任命されたときは、当然その地位を失ふ。

Article 103

The Ministers of State, members of the House of Representatives and judges in office on the effective date of this Constitution, and all other public officials who occupy positions corresponding to such positions as are recognized by this Constitution shall not forfeit their positions automatically on account of the enforcement of this Constitution unless otherwise specified by law. When, however, successors are elected or appointed under the provisions of this Constitution, they shall forfeit their positions as a matter of course.

1947年（昭和22年）。この年の5月3日、日本国憲法が施行される。江戸、明治、大正、昭和生まれと様々な世代が、全国で新しい憲法を祝福した。そして、やがては、生まれた時には既に憲法があったという人ばかりの時代が来る。その時も日本人はかつての感激を持ち続けて行くことができるだろうか。

——写真・共同通信社

1947 On 3 May, the Constitution of Japan became effective. People born in the Edo, Meiji, Taishō and Shōwa eras welcomed the new Constitution. It won't be long before everyone alive will have been born under this Constitution. When that time comes, will the strong sense of gratitude felt in 1947 still prevail?

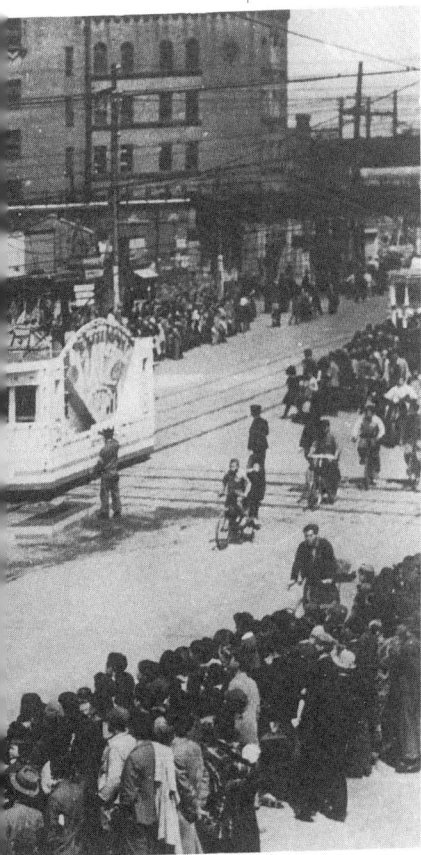

第2部・解説 日本国憲法

Part II • The Constitution of Japan: One View

メリーランド大学名誉教授
セオドア H. マックネリー

Theodore H. McNelly
Professor Emeritus, University of Maryland

はじめに

New Constitution
The Imperial Diet passed the Constitution Revision Bill.

A fireworks display celebrating the new Constitution and Diet (May 1947).

　日本国憲法は、大日本帝国憲法（明治憲法、1889年発布）に代わって、1947年5月3日に施行された。

　新憲法は、国民に主権が存在することを宣言し、基本的人権を擁護し、戦争と武力を放棄したことで注目された。

　民主主義に貫かれたこの憲法は、天皇に主権が存在するという原理に基づいていた旧憲法下での日本の政治体制を、革命的に変化させた。

INTRODUCTION

The Constitution of Japan (*Nihonkoku Kempō*), successor to the Constitution of the Empire of Japan (the *Meiji Constitution*, 1889), became effective on 3 May 1947.

It was notable for its declaration that sovereignty resided with the people, its assertion of fundamental human rights, and its renunciation of war and arms.

A thoroughly democratic document, it revolutionized the political system, which, under the preceding constitution, had been based on the principle that sovereignty resided with the emperor.

156

第1章　日本国憲法の制定

敗戦と憲法改正

　新憲法は、第2次世界大戦直後の連合国の日本占領中（1945-52年）に作成され、採択された。このため、外国からの強い影響を受けて制定されたものと一般に考えられている。

　第2次世界大戦中、アメリカ国務省では、日本の降伏と戦後の占領に関する政策が作成されていた。軍部による支配を終わらせ、政治的自由を守るためには、敗戦国日本の統治制度は根本的に変革されなければならないと、国務省では決めていた。

　しかし、天皇をその地位にとどめておくべきかどうか、また、どの程度の社会的・経済的改革を課すべきかについては、国務省内でも意見がまとまらず、これらについての最終的結論は、連合軍が東京で占領任務につくまで持ち越された。

　日本の降伏は、ポツダム宣言が求める条件の受諾という形で行われた。ポツダム宣言では、民主主義的傾向への障害の除去と、日本国民の自由に表明する意思に従って、平和を愛する政府が樹立されることを求めていた。

　天皇と日本国政府は、連合国最高司令官（略称SCAP）に従うことになっていた。

　ポツダム宣言や降伏文書は、帝国憲法の条文

The Potsdam Declaration was issued at Potsdam (near Berlin) on 26 July 1945, during the last Allied summit conference of World War II.

SCAP A term used to refer to both the chief executive of the Allied occupation of Japan and, as an acronym, his General Headquarters (GHQ) in Tōkyō.

CHAPTER 1 ENACTMENT OF THE CONSTITUTION

Defeat and Amendment of the Constitution

As the new constitution was formulated and adopted during the occupation (1945–52), it is generally believed to have been enacted under strong foreign influence.

During World War II, officials in the US Department of State had formulated policies concerning the surrender and postwar occupation of Japan. They had decided that the governmental system of the defeated country would have to be drastically reformed to end the dominance of the military and to protect political liberties.

They were unable to agree on whether or not the emperor should be retained and the extent of social and economic reform to be imposed, and they deferred final decision on these questions until after the Allied forces took charge in Tōkyō.

The Japanese surrender took the form of acceptance of the terms of the Potsdam Declaration, which called for the removal of obstacles to democratic tendencies and the establishment of a peace-loving government in accordance with the freely expressed will of the Japanese people.

The emperor and the government of Japan would be subject to the Supreme Commander for the Allied Powers (SCAP).

The textual amendment of the imperial constitution

158

の改正については、明確には触れていなかった。1945年8月14日［訳注：日本時間8月15日］に天皇が発した終戦の詔書は、戦争を終わらせるに当たって「国体」が護持されたと述べ、帝国としての法制度が守られたとの意味を含ませていた。

1945年10月、連合国最高司令官のダグラス・マッカーサー将軍は、当時、東久邇稔彦内閣の副総理を務めていた近衛文麿に、憲法を改正するのが望ましいと示唆した。また、マッカーサーは、その数日後、新首相の幣原喜重郎にも同じように伝えた。

General Douglas MacArthur arrives at Atsugi Air Base near Tōkyō on 30 August 1945 to serve as the Supreme Commander for the Allied Powers.

日本側の提案

近衛は、側近が連合国最高司令官政治顧問と接触を持っており、憲法改正の必要性について内大臣府に調査させるようにという委任を、天皇から受けた。

Konoe Fumimaro

近衛のこの動きは、国内外で批判された。その理由は、近衛自身に戦争責任の容疑があったこと（近衛は日中戦争［1937-1945］が始まった時の首相だった）、そして、憲法の改正は内大臣府ではなく内閣が取り扱うべき国事だったからである。

11月1日、連合国最高司令官総司令部（GHQ）は、近衛の努力を支持しないという声明を出した。しかし、その3週間後、近衛と、近衛の憲

was not explicitly mentioned in the Potsdam Declaration or the surrender documents. The emperor's surrender rescript of 14 August 1945 asserted that, in ending the war, the "structure of the imperial state" had been preserved, implying that the imperial institution had been saved.

In October 1945 General Douglas MacArthur, Supreme Commander for the Allied Powers, suggested to Konoe Fumimaro, then deputy premier in the Higashikuni Naruhiko cabinet, and a few days later to Prime Minister Shidehara Kijūrō the desirability of reforming the constitution.

Japanese Proposals

Konoe, whose advisers were in contact with the office of SCAP's political adviser, received from the emperor a commission to have the Office of the Lord Keeper of the Privy Seal (*Naidaijin Fu*) investigate the need for constitutional revision.

His action was criticized both in Japan and abroad because of his alleged war responsibility (Konoe had been prime minister when the Sino-Japanese War of 1937–1945 broke out) and because constitutional revision was a matter of state to be handled by the cabinet rather than by the Office of the Lord Keeper of the Privy Seal.

On 1 November, SCAP Headquarters issued a statement denying its sponsorship of the Konoe effort, but three weeks later Konoe and his chief associate,

法改正作業の中心的協力者だった佐々木惣一
は、それぞれ勧告を奉答書にまとめて天皇に報
告した。これらの奉答書は正式には発表されず、
その後の憲法草案に何も直接の影響を与えなか
った。

　内大臣府は、日本の戦時統治体制の中で非常
に強い力を持つようになっていたが、これらの
奉答書が提出された直後に廃止された。近衛は
12月、戦犯容疑で連合国側に収監される前夜に、
自殺した。

　マッカーサーからの憲法改正提案に対する、
幣原首相の当初の反応として伝えられたのは、
日本を民主化するという目的のために明治憲法
を改正する必要はない、というものだった。憲
法という国の基本法に手を加えなくても、女性
に投票権を与える新しい選挙法をはじめとする
適切な法律を制定すれば、民主化は実現できる
と、幣原は考えていた。

　とはいうものの、幣原は閣内からの要求に応
えて、優れた法律家で閣僚の一人だった松本烝
治を委員長に任命し、その委員会に憲法の改正
が必要かどうか、もし必要だとするとそれはど
の程度かを検討させることにした。

Shidehara Kijūrō

Matsumoto Jōji

Sasaki Sōichi, made separate reports to the throne on their recommendations. These reports were not formally published and had no direct influence on subsequent constitutional drafts.

Immediately after the reports were submitted, the Office of the Lord Keeper of the Privy Seal, which had become very powerful in the wartime government of Japan, was abolished. In December Konoe committed suicide on the night before he was due to be imprisoned by the Allies as a suspected war criminal.

Prime Minister Shidehara's initial publicized reaction to SCAP's suggestion of constitutional revision was that it was not necessary to revise the Meiji Constitution in order to democratize Japan. He believed that democratization could be accomplished without abusing that basic law by enacting appropriate legislation such as a new electoral law giving voting rights to women.

However, in response to the demand of his cabinet, he appointed Matsumoto Jōji, a prominent jurist and cabinet member, to head a committee to investigate whether the constitution needed revision and, if so, to what extent.

国務・陸軍・海軍三省調整委員会の方針

　1946年1月、ワシントンの国務・陸軍・海軍三省調整委員会(SWNCC—アメリカの対日占領政策を作った)で「日本統治体制の変革」についての方針(SWNCC-228)が採択され、GHQへ伝えられた。

　この文書では、行政府は、国民や選挙で選ばれた国民の代表者に対して直接に責任を負い、軍は文民の統制に従うべきものだとして、それを保証するためには、憲法の条文の変更が必要になることを、はっきりと述べていた。

GHQ-SCAP was part of the combined US headquarters that carried out both Allied responsibilities for the Occupation of Japan (GHQ-SCAP) and US military responsibilities throughout the Far East as General Headquarters, Far East Command (GHQ-FEC).

　天皇制を存続させるべきかどうかについては結論が出ていなかったが、もし皇位が残されるとすれば、天皇は、議会に責任を負うことになる内閣の助言と承認に基づいてのみ、行動が許されることになっていた。

　GHQ当局者には、公表されていた松本(烝治)の声明や、松本憲法私案の一つ(毎日新聞にスクープ掲載された)から、松本周辺の考えでは、三省調整委員会の求める条件に遠く及ばないことが、明らかだった。

　その一方では、連合国の占領政策を作成する機関として、新たに極東委員会が設けられ、委員会のメンバー諸国が、憲法の改正に強い関心を示していた。

State-War-Navy Coordinating Committee's Policy

In January 1946 the interdepartmental State-War-Navy Coordinating Committee in Washington (which made American policy for the occupation) adopted its policy on "The Reform of the Japanese Governmental System (SWNCC-228)," which was forwarded to SCAP Headquarters.

SWNCC-228 made it clear that textual changes in the constitution would be necessary in order to assure that the executive branch of the government would be responsible either directly to the people or to the people's elected representatives and that the military branch would be subordinate to the civilian branch of the government.

The question of whether or not the emperor system was to be preserved was left open, but if the throne was retained, the emperor should be permitted to act only on the advice of the cabinet, which would be responsible to the legislature.

It was clear to SCAP officials from Matsumoto's published statements and from one of his constitutional drafts (made public by the *Mainichi Shimbun*) that the Matsumoto group's ideas fell far short of SWNCC requirements.

In the meantime, members of the newly formed Far Eastern Commission (FEC), an Allied body set up to make Occupation policy, had shown keen interest in constitutional revision.

GHQ草案

　マッカーサーは、極東委員会が機能し始める
と自身の行動の自由が大きく損なわれると判断
し、GHQ 民政局に、幣原内閣の指針となるよ
うなモデル憲法案を起草するよう命令した。

　民政局が慌ただしく用意した憲法草案は、あ
る程度は SWNCC-228 に基づいていたが、そ
れよりはむしろ、起草したアメリカ人スタッフ
のリベラルな民主主義の理想に多くを負ってい
た。この草案は、天皇は日本国の象徴であり日
本国民統合の象徴であると述べ、国民主権の原
則と、戦争と武力の放棄を宣言していた。

　1946年 2 月13日、民政局当局者は GHQ 草案
を日本政府に届けた。そして、この草案に盛り
込まれている基本原則が受け入れられなけれ
ば、連合国最高司令官には、天皇を戦争犯罪人
として裁かれることから守るのが難しくなると
警告した。

　その後の高官レベルでの折衝と、民政局と日
本政府間での徹夜の緊密な共同作業を経て、
GHQ 草案にのっとった日本側の憲法草案が合
意された。GHQ が日本側の見解に示した唯一
の大きな譲歩は、民政局の草案では一院制と決
められていた国会が、二院制にされたことだけ
だった。

政府の改正草案

　1946年 3 月 6 日、幣原内閣はこの草案を自前
のものとして公表した。しかし、この草案にこ

Tōkyō Trial

The SCAP Draft

MacArthur, aware that his freedom to act would be greatly inhibited by the FEC when that body began its work, directed his Government Section (GS) to draft a model constitution as a guide for the Shidehara cabinet.

The Government Section's hastily drafted constitution was based in part on SWNCC-228 but owed much to the liberal democratic ideals of its American authors. It stated that the emperor was the symbol of the state and of the unity of the people and declared the principle of popular sovereignty and the renunciation of war and arms.

On 13 February 1946, GS officials delivered the SCAP draft to the Japanese cabinet with the warning that failure to adopt its basic principles would make it difficult for SCAP to protect the emperor from trial as a war criminal.

After further high-level negotiation and an overnight session of close collaboration between GS and Japanese officials, a Japanese draft constitution based on the SCAP model was agreed upon. The only major concession to Japanese views was that the Diet be bicameral, rather than unicameral as provided in the GS draft.

The Government's Revision Bill

On 6 March 1946 the Shidehara cabinet published the text as its own handiwork, although in spirit and detail

められた精神や細部の表現は、もとの松本私案とはまったく違っていた。

この憲法草案は、憲法の改正を支持するという天皇の勅語とともに発表された。これにより、皇位を廃止すべきかどうか、また、その座にある者を戦争犯罪人として裁くべきかどうかに関する国際的な論争に、ほぼ終止符が打たれた。

マッカーサーにとって天皇は、日本を統治する上できわめて貴重な存在になっていた。天皇は、1946年1月1日の詔書で自身が神であることを否定したのに続いて、憲法の改正を支持した。それにより、天皇は、日本の民主化に積極的な役割を果たす力として現れていた。

3月6日のこの草案は、政府が4月17日に発表した憲法改正草案の基礎にされた。この改正草案は、法律文書で伝統的に使われていた文語体でなく、口語の文法で書かれていたことで注目された。

幣原首相は、この憲法草案を枢密院に提出した。枢密院には、その組織を定めた勅令により、憲法に関わる法律を審議する権限が与えられていたからである。

主権の所在、皇室財政、武力放棄を中心に戦わされた激しい議論の末、全会一致ではなかったものの、枢密院は6月8日にこの憲法草案を承認した。

草案に国会で変更が加えられたあと、10月29

Emperor Shōwa
(1901–89)
Emperor Shōwa
visits General
Douglas MacArthur
on 27 September
1945.

it differed radically from the previous Matsumoto proposals.

The publication of the draft constitution, together with a statement by the emperor indicating his sponsorship of constitutional revision, largely brought to an end the international debate as to whether or not the throne should be abolished or its occupant tried as a war criminal.

The emperor had become invaluable to MacArthur in the governing of Japan. By renouncing his divinity in his 1 January 1946 rescript and by sponsoring constitutional revision, the emperor had emerged as a positive force in the democratization of Japan.

The 6 March draft was made the basis of the government's Constitution Revision Bill of 17 April, which was notable for being written in colloquial grammar rather than in the formal style traditionally used in legal documents.

Prime Minister Shidehara submitted the proposed constitution to the Privy Council, which, under its organizational ordinance, was empowered to deliberate on laws relating to the constitution.

Following emotion-charged discussions focusing on the location of sovereignty, imperial household finances, and the renunciation of arms, the Privy Council approved, although not unanimously, the draft constitution on 8 June.

Following changes in the bill made by the Diet, the

日に、枢密院はふたたび草案を承認した(新憲
法に定められていなかった枢密院は、1947年に
廃止された)。

帝国議会での審議

　憲法改正草案の国会審議は、1946年の夏に行
われた。審議の過程で、吉田茂首相と、憲法草
案の国会への説明を担当していた金森徳次郎国
務大臣は、この新憲法草案を制定することは、
皇位を存続させ、連合国側が占領終了のために
求めている第一の条件を満たすことになるのだ
と強調した。

　両院での審議で主な論点として取り上げられ
たのは、国民主権、「日本国の象徴であり日本
国民統合の象徴」であるという天皇の新しい地
位、皇室財産の処置、戦争と武装の放棄の諸原
則だった。

　極東委員会は、この時期にマッカーサーに宛
てた指令の中で、国民主権と皇室財産の国有化
の規定を強めるよう求めた。また、閣僚は全員
文民とし、その過半数は国会議員の中から任命
されるという規定を入れるよう主張した。民政
局は、極東委員会のこの要望が確実に織り込ま
れるよう、日本政府や国会議員と何度か秘密会
議を行った。

Privy Council again approved it on 29 October. (The Privy Council, which was not provided for in the new constitution, was abolished in 1947.)

Deliberations in the Imperial Diet

During the Diet deliberations on the Constitution Revision Bill in the summer of 1946, Prime Minister Yoshida Shigeru and Minister of State Kanamori Tokujirō, who was charged with explaining the draft constitution to the Diet, emphasized that the enactment of the proposed new constitution would preserve the throne and would meet a principal Allied requirement for terminating the occupation.

The main points raised in the deliberations in the two houses were the principles of popular sovereignty, the new position of the emperor as "symbol of the state and of the unity of the people," the disposition of the property of the imperial household, and the renunciation of war and armaments.

The Far Eastern Commission insisted in its instructions to MacArthur at this time that the provisions relating to popular sovereignty and the nationalization of imperial property be strengthened, and that provisions be inserted that all cabinet ministers be civilians and that the majority of them be appointed from the Diet. GS officers held secret conferences with government officials and with Diet members in order to ensure the adoption of the FEC desiderata.

新憲法の制定

　憲法改正草案は、帝国議会の両院でほぼ全会一致で可決され、旧憲法の第73条に従って、旧憲法を改正するという形で新憲法が制定された。1946年11月3日（明治天皇の誕生日）に裕仁天皇により公布された日本国憲法は、翌1947年の5月3日に施行された。旧憲法との法律的継続性がこうして保たれた。

Emperor Meiji
(1852–1912)
Succeeding to the throne in 1867 at the age of 14, Emperor Meiji became the symbolic focus of the movement to overthrow the Tokugawa shogunate.

　民主主義と平和主義を掲げた新憲法の規定が、日本の伝統からあまりにもかけ離れていたこと、また、GHQがこの憲法を日本国民に"押しつけた"という見方から、事態を見守ってきた人々の間には、新憲法は、占領の終わりまでは多分持たないだろうという意見も多かった。

　新憲法が公布される直前の1946年10月、極東委員会は、1948年の5月3日から1949年の5月3日の間に、日本の国会と同委員会とで「憲法に関する状況を見直す」ことを決定した。憲法に関する日本国民の意見を確かめるためには、国民投票などの手続きが必要になるかもしれない、と極東委員会は述べた。

　マッカーサー将軍は、極東委員会のこの方針に強く反対した。これでは、憲法が施行もされない前に、その法的地位を損なうことになりかねない、また、新憲法の規定により国会と国民は既にどのような変更も自由に行えるのだから、こうした手続きは不要だと思われる、とい

Enacting the New Constitution

The Constitution Revision Bill was passed almost unanimously by both houses of the Imperial Diet, so that the new constitution was enacted in the form of an amendment to the old constitution in accordance with Article 73 of the latter document. Promulgated by Emperor Hirohito on 3 November 1946 (the birthday of Emperor Meiji), the Constitution of Japan became effective on 3 May 1947. Legal continuity with the old constitution was thus assured.

Because the democratic and pacifist provisions of the new constitution stood in such dramatic contrast to Japanese traditions and because of the belief that SCAP Headquarters had "imposed" it on the Japanese, many observers believed that the new constitution would probably not outlast the Occupation

In October 1946, shortly before the new constitution was promulgated, the FEC decided that both the Diet and the commission would, between 3 May 1948 and 3 May 1949, "review the situation with respect to the constitution." The commission stated that it might require a referendum or other procedure to ascertain Japanese opinion of the constitution.

General MacArthur strongly objected to this policy, believing that it might undermine the legal status of the constitution even before it became effective and that it seemed unnecessary, since the Diet and the people were already free under the provisions of the constitution to make any changes.

うのが、彼の考えだった。

　マッカーサーが、極東委員会の見直しの方針を日本政府に知らせるのを拒むと、同委員会は、この方針を公表するとマッカーサーに迫った。（マッカーサー将軍は極東委員会の方針を私信で吉田首相に伝えた。）

　極東委員会の見直し政策に触れる報道は、GHQ の命令により、検閲ですべて削除された。国会は、憲法を見直すための公式の手続きを何も取らなかった。国民投票も行われず、極東委員会は、予定していた期間中に、憲法のごく形式的な見直しをしただけであった。

When he refused to inform the Japanese government of the FEC review policy, the commission threatened to make the policy public. (The general conveyed the FEC policy in a private letter to Prime Minister Yoshida.)

All references to the FEC review policy were censored from the Japanese press by order of SCAP, and the Diet made no formal move to review the constitution. No referendum was held, and the FEC made only a very perfunctory review of the constitution in the prescribed period.

日本国憲法の諸原則

国民主権

日本国憲法の第 1 章第 1 条は、天皇は「日本国の象徴であり日本国民統合の象徴であつて、この地位は、主権の存する日本国民の総意に基く」と宣言している。

法律学者の間には、天皇から国民への主権の移行は、この新憲法の制定以前、すなわち日本政府がポツダム宣言の条件を受諾した時点で、既に行われていたとする説もある。

天皇は、自身が神であるという考えをすでに放棄し、その結果、明治憲法下での主権者としての権威を支えていた超自然的な基盤を否定してしまっていた。

天皇が政治的主権者として日本を支配するという理論は、もともとは、8 世紀から 9 世紀の日本に大きな影響を与えた中国型の皇帝統治に基づいており、その理論が、明治時代 (1868-1912年) にドイツの影響を受けてふたたび主張され、近代化されたものだった。

法制史研究者の間には、日本国の象徴であり日本国民統合の象徴であるという天皇の現在の地位は、明治憲法が基づいている天皇主権論よりも日本の固有の伝統にかなっていると主張す

Surrender Ceremony
The official World War II surrender ceremony aboard the USS *Missouri* on 2 September 1945.

San Francisco Peace Treaty
On 8 September 1951, Prime Minister Shigeru Yoshida signs the treaty that ended the formal state of war between Japan and the non-Communist Allied powers.

CHAPTER 2

**PRINCIPLES OF
THE CONSTITUTION**

Popular Sovereignty

Chapter I, Article 1 of the Constitution of Japan
declares that the emperor shall be "the symbol of the
State and of the unity of the people, deriving his position from the will of the people with whom resides
sovereign power."

According to some legal scholars, the transfer of
sovereignty from the emperor to the people had already
occurred before the enactment of the new constitution,
when the Japanese government accepted the terms of
the Potsdam Declaration.

The emperor had renounced the concept of his
divinity, thus denying the supernatural basis of his sovereign authority under the Meiji Constitution.

The theory that the emperor was the politically sovereign ruler of Japan had originally been based on the
Chinese model of imperial government, which had
greatly influenced Japan in the 8th and 9th centuries,
and this theory had been reaffirmed and modernized as
the result of German influence during the Meiji period
(1868–1912).

Some legal historians assert that the present status
of the emperor as symbol of the state and of national
unity is more in harmony with indigenous Japanese
tradition than was the theory of imperial sovereignty

る説もある。

「象徴」としての天皇

　国事に関する天皇の行為は、新憲法ではすべて内閣の助言と承認を必要とし、天皇は「国政に関する権能」を持っていない。

　天皇は国会が選んだ者を首相に任命し、内閣が指名した者を最高裁判所の長たる裁判官に任命する。内閣の助言と承認により、天皇は憲法の改正と法律・政令・条約を公布し、国会を召集し、衆議院を解散し、総選挙の施行を公示し、国務大臣と外交官の任命を認証し、恩赦を認証し、栄典を授与し、条約の批准を認証し、外国の外交官を接受し、儀式を執り行う。

　皇位は世襲制で、国会が可決した皇室典範に従って継承される（旧皇室典範は1889年に明治憲法と同時に公布され、明治憲法から独立して存在していた）。

　明治憲法下では、日本の官僚と軍部の権威は、天皇から直接または間接的に任命されているということに由来していた。新憲法下での公務員は、天皇ではなく、国民を代表する国会と内閣の統制下に置かれた。

Emperor Akihito (1933–)
Accompanied by Empress Michiko, Emperor Akihito welcomes US President Bill Clinton and his wife Hillary Rodham Clinton to Japan.

enunciated in the Meiji Constitution.

The Emperor as a "Symbol"

All acts of the emperor in matters of state now require the advice and approval of the cabinet, and the emperor has no "powers related to government."

The emperor appoints as prime minister the person selected by the Diet and appoints as chief judge of the Supreme Court the appointee of the cabinet. With the advice and approval of the cabinet he promulgates constitutional amendments, laws, cabinet orders, and treaties; convokes the Diet; dissolves the House of Representatives; proclaims general elections; attests the appointment of cabinet ministers and diplomats; attests amnesties; awards honors; attests ratifications of treaties; receives foreign diplomats; and performs ceremonial functions.

The throne is dynastic and is transmitted in accordance with the Imperial Household Law passed by the Diet. (The old Imperial Household Law had been promulgated in 1889, simultaneously with the Meiji Constitution, and had existed independently of the latter document.)

Under the Meiji Constitution, the Japanese bureaucracy and military had derived their authority from the fact of their direct or indirect appointment by the emperor. Under the new constitution, the civil service was placed under the control of the Diet and cabinet, representing the people, rather than the emperor.

178

　新しい平和主義憲法では、天皇の軍事的な役
割について、何も触れていなかった。天皇の統
帥権は、かつては、首相や内閣による統制から
の独立を主張しようとする陸海軍の上層部に利
用されていた。

　新憲法では、天皇の権威が大きく制限されて
いる一方で、国民の主権が非常に強調されてい
るので、日本は君主制ではないと主張する意見
もある。皇位を廃止するよう憲法を改正するこ
とは、法的には可能に見える。しかしまた、天
皇を国家の象徴ではなく、国家元首の地位に戻
すことも、法的には可能に思われる。

　日本の統治制度の中での天皇の役割は、新憲
法の条文に示されているより、はるかに微妙で
複雑である。皇室の成員が持つ独特の特権と責
任は、憲法に述べられている人間の平等の原理
とは矛盾している。一部の法律解説者が言うよ
うに、天皇をもし国民の中に含めるとすると、
主権が天皇から国民へ移ったという理論は、一
見してそう見えるよりは、はるかに革命性が薄
いことになる。

　天皇が国務を執行しているとき、はたして内
閣の助言を受け取ったり、受け入れたりできな
いような、緊急事態が起きることはないのだろ
うか？
　日本国の象徴であり日本国民統合の象徴であ
るという天皇の役割は、危機的な状況の中では、

No mention was made in the new pacifist constitution of a military role for the emperor, whose military prerogative (*tōsuiken*) had formerly been used by the army and navy high commands to assert their independence of control by the prime minister and cabinet.

The authority of the emperor is so circumscribed and the people's sovereignty so emphasized under the new constitution that some writers assert that Japan is not a monarchy. It appears legally possible to amend the constitution so as to abolish the throne, just as it seems legally possible to restore the emperor to the position of head of the state, rather than symbol of the state.

The role of the emperor in the Japanese political system is far more subtle and complex than is suggested by the terms of the new constitution. The unique privileges and responsibilities of the members of the imperial family contradict the principle of human equality enunciated by the constitution. If one includes the emperor among the people, as do some commentators, the theory that sovereignty has been transferred from the emperor to the people is much less revolutionary than it might at first seem.

Might there not arise emergencies in which the emperor, in the performance of his duties, would be unable to receive or to accept the advice of the cabinet?

Does not the emperor's role as symbol of the state and of national unity imply in practice some degree,

あるいは決定的な意味を持ちかねない一定程度（たとえその程度は曖昧だとしても）の、実質的な政治的権力を、現実には意味しないのだろうか？

　天皇が政治的に中立でいることは、本当に可能なのだろうか？　天皇が国民の前に姿をあらわせば、なにがしかのグループからほとんどかならず、政府が天皇の権威を利用しているという、不満が出ることになる。

不戦非武装の規定

　日本国憲法の最も有名な規定は、第2章の「戦争の放棄」であり、その全文は次のように書かれている。

第9条

　日本国民は、正義と秩序を基調とする国際平和を誠実に希求し、国権の発動たる戦争と、武力による威嚇又は武力の行使は、国際紛争を解決する手段としては、永久にこれを放棄する。

　②前項の目的を達するため、陸海空軍その他の戦力は、これを保持しない。国の交戦権は、これを認めない。

　マッカーサー将軍は、この規定は、1946年1月に幣原首相から提案されたものだと、1951年に述べた。しかし、日本の権威筋には、幣原首相が、この憲法により日本が永久に非武装化さ

Zero fighter
The range and maneuverability of the Zero made it the mainstay of Japan's naval air forces and one of the most famous fighter planes of World War II.

however vague, of substantive political power, which might prove decisive in crucial situations?

Is it really possible for the emperor to be politically neutral? The emperor can scarcely make a public appearance without some group or another complaining about the use the government is making of his prestige.

The No-War, No-Arms Provision

The most famous provision of the Constitution of Japan is Chapter II, "Renunciation of War," which, in its entirety, reads:

Article 9

Aspiring sincerely to an international peace based on justice and order, the Japanese people forever renounce war as a sovereign right of the nation and the threat or use of force as means of settling international disputes.

(2) In order to accomplish the aim of the preceding paragraph, land, sea, and air forces, as well as other war potential, will never be maintained. The right of belligerency of the state will not be recognized.

General MacArthur asserted in 1951 that this provision had been suggested to him by Prime Minister Shidehara in January 1946, but some Japanese authorities doubt whether Shidehara intended that Japan

れることを本当に意図していたかどうかを疑う
意見がある。この条項の厳密な解釈については
広範な論議が行われ、自衛隊と日米安全保障条
約の合憲性を判断するときの基礎になってき
た。

　日本政府と保守勢力の大半は、第9条の第1
項は自衛のための戦争を放棄したものではな
く、また、第2項の武装禁止は「前項の目的を
達するため」と限定されているので、防衛的な
軍備は禁止されていないという見解を取ってき
た。さらに政府は、自衛隊の合憲性は裁判所の
司法審査権の範囲を超える"政治問題"だと主張
してきた。

　世論調査では、日本国民の過半数が第9条の
どのような改正にも反対しているという結果が
つねに示されてきた。また、自衛隊の合憲性に
ついては議論の余地があるものの、国民は自衛
隊が引き続き維持されるのを望んでいることも
示されている。

権利の章典

　新憲法第3章の「国民の権利及び義務」は、
明治憲法第2章の「臣民権利義務」とは、際立
った対照を示している。

　旧憲法は、「安寧秩序を妨げず、及び臣民た
るの義務に背かざる限りに於いて」信教の自由
の権利を与えていた［訳注：旧憲法は片仮名を平

should be permanently disarmed by the constitution. The precise interpretation of this clause has been widely debated, and it has been the basis of tests of the constitutionality of the Self Defense Forces and of the United States-Japan security treaties.

The view of the Japanese government and most conservatives has been that paragraph 1 of Article 9 does not renounce wars of self-defense and that the ban on armaments in paragraph 2 is qualified by the phrase "in order to accomplish the aim of the preceding paragraph," so that defensive armament is not forbidden. Furthermore, the government has asserted that the constitutionality of the Self Defense Forces is a "political question" beyond the scope of the courts' power of judicial review.

Public opinion polls have consistently shown that the majority of the Japanese people oppose any amendment to Article 9. They also show that the public favors the continued maintenance of the Self Defense Forces, in spite of their debatable constitutionality.

The Bill of Rights

Chapter III of the new constitution, on the "Rights and Duties of the People," contrasts sharply with Chapter II, "Rights and Duties of Subjects," of the Meiji Constitution.

The old basic law conferred the right of freedom of religious belief "within limits not prejudicial to peace and order, and not antagonistic to their [the people's]

仮名に変え、必要に応じて送り仮名や濁点をつけた]。一方、新憲法は、信教の自由をはっきりと保障し、いかなる「宗教上の行為、祝典、儀式又は行事」への強制的参加も禁止し、国が宗教教育その他のいかなる宗教的活動を助けることも禁じている。

旧憲法は、日本臣民は言論・著作・印行・集会・結社の自由を「法律の範囲内に於いて」持つと定めていた。これに対して、新憲法は法律によって表現の自由を制限することを認めず、検閲を明確に禁止し、通信の秘密を保護している。

この第3章は、憲法の原案を起草したアメリカ人スタッフの、リベラルな政治理念を反映しているように見える。例えば、「人種、信条、性別、社会的身分又は門地により、政治的、経済的又は社会的関係において」差別することは禁止されている。選挙は普通選挙である。男女は配偶者の選択、財産権、相続、住居の選定、離婚並びに婚姻及び家族に関するその他の事項について、法律的に平等の権利を持つ。教育は義務教育で、無償である。裁判を受ける被告人が持つ幅広い権利についても、詳細に定めている。この憲法は、国民が「健康で文化的な最低限度の生活」を営む権利を持ち、国は社会福祉、社会保障、公衆衛生を増進させなければならないと定めている。

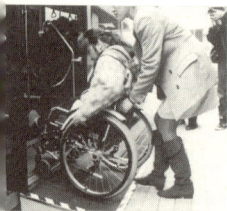

A bus with special equipment for a wheelchair user.

duties as subjects," whereas the new constitution flatly guarantees freedom of religion, forbids compulsory participation in any "religious act, celebration, rite or practice," and prohibits the state from supporting religious education or any other religious activity.

The old constitution provided that Japanese subjects should enjoy liberty of speech, writing, publication, public meetings and associations "within the limits of the law," whereas the new basic law does not authorize legal limitations on freedom of expression but explicitly bans censorship and protects the secrecy of communications.

Chapter III appears to reflect the political liberalism of the Americans who originally drafted it. For example, discrimination "in political, economic or social relations because of race, creed, sex, social status or family origin" is banned. Suffrage is universal. Men and women have legal equality in choice of spouse, in property rights, inheritance, choice of domicile, divorce and other matters pertaining to marriage and the family. Education is compulsory and free. Extensive rights of the accused in trials are elaborately spelled out. The constitution provides that the people have the right to maintain "minimum standards of wholesome and cultured living" and that the state will promote social welfare and security and public health.

日本国憲法は、人種間や男女の平等にかかわる事柄については、アメリカ憲法よりはるかに進歩的である。しかしながら、そのニューディール的な色彩にもかかわらず、日本の憲法は、日本の社会主義者や共産主義者が主張していた経済権・社会権を個別に列挙することはしていない。

新憲法は社会主義的なものではないが、「財産権は、これを侵してはならない」としている他には、国の持つ公用収用権に基づき、政府が社会主義的な政策を立法化することを禁止していない。

国の立法府

国会について定めた第4章では、この機関が「国権の最高機関」で、「国の唯一の立法機関」であると宣言されている。

新憲法の立案者たちは、国政の中心を占めるのは軍国主義者や官僚ではなく、選挙で選ばれた国民の代表者でなければならないと決めていた。

国会は衆議院と参議院からなり、略してそれぞれ下院、上院と呼ばれることが多い［訳注：日本語では、日本の両院について、下院、上院という呼び方は一般的でない。以下ではそれぞれ衆議院、参議院とする］。衆議院議員の任期は4年だが、ふつうは衆議院の解散にともなってその前に終了する。参議院議員の任期は6年だが、半数ずつずれている。すなわち、3年ごとに議席の半

National Diet
Completed in 1936, the Diet Building has an exterior of domestic granite.

The Japanese constitution is far more progressive than the American in matters of ethnic and sexual equality. Despite its New Dealish tone, however, the Japanese document omits a long list of specific economic and social rights that were advocated by Japanese socialists and communists.

The new constitution is not socialist, but it does not forbid the government to enact socialistic policies, except that "the right to own or to hold property is inviolable," subject to the state's right of eminent domain.

The National Legislature

In Chapter IV, on the Diet, that body is declared to be "the highest organ of state power" and "the sole law-making organ of the State."

The framers of the new constitution were determined that the people's elected representatives, rather than militarists or bureaucrats, should prevail in the government of the nation.

The Diet consists of the House of Representatives and the House of Councillors, often informally referred to as the lower house and upper house, respectively. The term of office of the representatives is four years, although it usually ends sooner than that, when the House is dissolved. The councillors' terms run for six years staggered, meaning that half the seats fall vacant once every three years.

分が改選になる。

　両議院の議員及びその選挙人の資格は、法律で定めることになっているが、「人種、信条、性別、社会的身分、門地、教育、財産又は収入によつて差別してはならない」とされている。この差別禁止規定があるため、一方の議院を職能代表制にすること、つまり、地理的に決められた選挙区ではなく、様々な経済的・社会的集団を代表するような選挙法や国会法を制定することは、違憲とみなされてきた。国会の両院の政治構成は、国会が可決する選挙法の規定に大きく左右される。

　法律案（予算または条約以外の）は、両議院で可決されたときに法律となる。しかし、衆議院が可決した法律案を参議院が否決ないしは修正を加えて可決したときは、衆議院は３分の２以上の多数でその法律案を再可決することによって、参議院の拒否権を無効にすることができる。

　予算または条約が衆議院で可決され、参議院がそれを否決ないしは修正可決したり、30日以内に議決しないときは、衆議院の議決が優先する。

　参議院に対する衆議院の優位は絶対的ではない。内閣は参議院を解散する権限を持っていない。内閣が、参議院の拒否ないしは修正可決権を無効とするために必要な３分の２の多数を衆議院で確保していない場合は、内閣が提出した重要な法律案が参議院で阻止されることもあり

Blocking the Passage of a Controversial Bill
Politicians stage a sit-in in the Diet.

Qualifications for members of both houses and for the voters are to be fixed by law, but there must be "no discrimination because of race, creed, sex, social status, family origin, education, property or income." Because of this nondiscrimination provision, it has been regarded as unconstitutional to enact any electoral law or Diet law that would make one chamber functional, that is, representative of various economic and social groups rather than geographic districts. The political composition of both houses of the Diet depends largely on the provisions of the electoral laws which the Diet passes.

Bills (other than the budget or treaties) become law when passed by both houses. However, if the councillors defeat a bill passed by the representatives, the latter may override the councillors' veto by repassing the bill with a two-thirds majority.

When a budget or treaty is passed by the lower house and the upper house defeats it or fails to act within 30 days, the decision of the lower house prevails.

The primacy of the lower house over the upper is not absolute. The cabinet does not have the power to dissolve the House of Councillors. In the event that the cabinet does not command the two-thirds majority in the lower house necessary to override an upper house veto, important cabinet bills can be blocked by the

うる。

　その場合、内閣は、法律案の否決を受け入れるか、野党側と交渉し、法案の修正を受け入れる譲歩をしたりしなければならないだろう。

　帝国議会が1947年に制定した国会法は、新憲法下での国会の組織と権限をかなり詳細に定めている。

内　閣

　憲法の第5章は内閣を扱っている。

　内閣総理大臣は国会の議決により指名される。衆議院と参議院が、その指名について意見が一致しないときは、衆議院の議決が優先する。天皇は国会が指名した者を内閣総理大臣に任命する。内閣総理大臣は、ほかの閣僚を任命し、罷免する。閣僚は全員が文民で、その過半数は国会議員でなければならない。

Prime Minister's
Official Residence

　内閣は、国会に対して連帯して責任を負う。衆議院が内閣不信任の決議案を可決したとき（または、信任の決議案を否決したとき）は、内閣は総辞職するか、10日以内に衆議院が解散されなくてはならない。天皇は内閣の助言と承認により衆議院を解散する。その場合は、解散から40日以内に総選挙が行われなければならない。

　憲法では、不信任の投票（第69条）が先になくても内閣が解散（第7条）を行えるかどうかは、明らかにされていない。言うまでもなく、

upper house.

The cabinet may then have to accept the defeat of the bill or negotiate a compromise with the opposition, possibly by accepting amendments to the bill.

The Diet Law, enacted by the Imperial Diet in 1947, spells out in considerable detail the organization and functioning of the Diet under the new constitution.

The Cabinet

Chapter V of the constitution concerns the cabinet.

The prime minister is designated by a resolution passed by the Diet. If the House of Representatives and the House of Councillors cannot agree on a choice, the decision of the representatives prevails. The emperor appoints as prime minister the person designated by the Diet. The prime minister selects and dismisses the other cabinet ministers, all of whom must be civilians and a majority of whom must be Diet members.

The cabinet is collectively responsible to the Diet. If the House of Representatives passes a resolution of no confidence (or rejects a resolution of confidence) in the cabinet, either the cabinet must resign en masse or the House of Representatives must be dissolved within ten days. The emperor, on the advice and approval of the cabinet, dissolves the House of Representatives. A general election must be held within 40 days after a dissolution.

The constitution is unclear as to whether or not the cabinet may bring about a dissolution (Article 7) without there first being a vote of no confidence (Article

もし内閣がいつでも好きな時に衆議院を解散できるとすると、内閣は解散の脅しを武器に使って、憲法が「国権の最高機関」と呼んでいる国会を威嚇することができ、内閣にとって政治的に有利な時に衆議院選挙を行えることになる。

1952年に吉田内閣は、事前に不信任の投票がないのに衆議院を解散した。それにより任期を短縮された一議員が、この件を最高裁判所に提訴した。最高裁は、内閣の取った手続きには変則的な点があるとしながらも、この申し立ては司法判断になじまず、裁判所は何もできないと判決した。それ以来、内閣は最大限の裁量を行使して解散権を利用してきた。

Yoshida Shigeru

1955年から1993年までの40年近くのあいだ、自由民主党が衆議院の議席の過半数と内閣総理大臣の座を占めてきた。そのため、自民党が一つにまとまっているかぎりにおいては、自民党内閣への不信任投票を阻止することができた。

自民党に対抗する政党が最大の争点として用いてきたのは、自民党が改憲を唱えているということであり、保守勢力は憲法の改正に必要とされる国会の両院での3分の2の多数を、一度も獲得出来なかった。

自民党から多数の党員が離党したあとで行われた1993年の衆議院選挙で、自民党は議会での多数を失った。そして、その翌年には、自民党員が多数を占める連立内閣で、社会民主党［訳注：就任当時は社会党委員長］の村山富市が首相

69). Obviously, if the cabinet may dissolve the lower house whenever it pleases, it can use the threat of dissolution as a weapon to intimidate the Diet, which the constitution calls "the highest organ of state power," and the cabinet can hold lower-house elections at times that are politically advantageous to it.

In 1952 the Yoshida cabinet dissolved the lower house without a prior vote of no confidence. A representative whose term of office was thus shortened appealed the matter to the Supreme Court, which found that although there were irregularities in the cabinet's procedure, the case was not justiciable and the court could do nothing. Since then, the cabinet has exercised full discretion in using the power of dissolution.

From 1955 to 1993—nearly four decades—the Liberal Democratic Party (LDP) held the majority of seats in the House of Representatives and the premiership. Thus, so long as the LDP remained united, it could prevent a vote of no confidence in an LDP cabinet.

A principal issue used by political parties campaigning against the LDP was the LDP's advocacy of constitutional revision, and the conservatives were never able to win the two-thirds of the seats in both houses of the Diet needed to amend the constitution.

In the 1993 lower house election, following the secession of many of its members, the LDP lost its parliamentary majority. In the following year Murayama Tomiichi, a Social-Democrat, became prime minister of a coalition cabinet in which the majority of minis-

になった。

1997年の日本は、自民党の首相の指導下にもどっている。しかし、自民党は国会での多数を欠いており、政党の再編と新しい選挙制度の実施によって、憲法の改革は以前ほどには目立たない争点になった。

裁判所

司法府については憲法の第6章に述べられている。

最高裁判所は、内閣が指名して天皇が任命する長たる裁判官と、法律の定める員数の裁判官からなり、長たる裁判官以外の裁判官は内閣により任命される。（1947年に公布された裁判所法は、最高裁判所の裁判官の員数を、長たる裁判官を含めて15人に定めた）。

最高裁判所の裁判官は、任命後最初に行われる衆議院選挙で、有権者の審査を受け、その後も10年ごとに再審査される。実際には、裁判官が有権者の審査で拒否されそうになったことはこれまでない。

下級裁判所の裁判官は、最高裁が提出する名簿から、内閣により任命される。日本には地方別の裁判所制度はなく、すべての裁判所が一つの全国的な制度に属している。

日本の裁判所が持つ権限で最も注目に値するのは、法律・命令・規則・処分が憲法に適合するかどうかを決定する権限が、憲法で裁判所に与えられていることであろう。このように、日

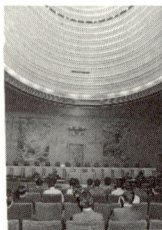

The Supreme Court in a grand bench session, which requires the presence of at least nine court justices. Most cases are not examined by the grand bench, but by one of the three petty benches into which it is divided.

ters were LDP members.

By 1997, Japan was again led by an LDP prime minister, but the LDP lacked majorities in the Diet, and the restructuring of the political parties and the implementation of a new electoral system reduced constitutional reform to a less salient issue.

The Courts

The judiciary is described in Chapter VI of the constitution.

The Supreme Court consists of a chief judge, designated by the cabinet and appointed by the emperor, and such number of judges as determined by law, who are appointed by the cabinet. (The Court Organization Law of 1947 prescribed a total of 15 judges, including the chief judge in the Supreme Court.)

At the first lower-house election after the appointment of a Supreme Court judge, the appointment is subject to review by the voters, and it is again reviewed at ten-year intervals thereafter. In practice, no judge has ever come close to being rejected by the voters.

Judges of inferior courts are appointed by the cabinet from a list submitted by the Supreme Court. There are no local systems of courts in Japan; all the courts belong to a single national system.

Perhaps the most notable power of the courts in Japan is the authority granted to them by the constitution to determine the constitutionality of laws, orders, regulations, and official acts. Thus the Japanese consti-

本の憲法は、アメリカでは合衆国憲法に明記されないままに裁判所が行使している違憲審査の権限を、条文により裁判所にはっきりと委ねている。

その他の重要な規定

財　政

新憲法の財政の扱い（第7章）は、戦前の財政制度と根本的な違いを示している。

政府予算案が国会で否決された際、政府にはもはや、かつてのように前年度の予算を施行することはできない。新憲法下では、国会の承認なしに税を課したり、国費を支出することはできない。皇室財産は国に属し、皇室の費用は予算に計上し、国会で議決される。皇室はこのように、もはや財政的な独立性を持っていない。

地方自治

地方自治について定めた第8章は、「地方自治の本旨」をうたっている。

しかし、地方公共団体の組織と権限は、憲法では定められていない。それらは、法律、すなわち国会が可決した成文法で決められる。このため、地方公共団体が果たすことのできる機能は、国会が地方公共団体に委ねることにしたものだけである。

Tōkyō Metropolitan Government Offices
This new landmark and symbol of Japan's capital city was completed in 1991.

tution explicitly delegates to the courts a power that is exercised by American courts without the explicit authorization of the US Constitution.

Other Important Provisions

Finance

The treatment of finance in the new constitution (Chapter VII) represents a radical break with the pre-war financial system.

The government is no longer able, as in the past, to enforce the budget of the preceding year if its proposed budget is defeated in the Diet. Under the new basic law, taxes cannot be imposed nor funds expended without the approval of the Diet. The imperial household property belongs to the state, and the expenses of the imperial household are appropriated by the Diet in the budget. The imperial household is thus no longer financially independent.

Local Self-Government

Chapter VIII, on local self-government, declares "the principle of local autonomy."

However, the organization and powers of local governments are not enumerated in the constitution but are determined by law, that is, statutes passed by the Diet. Local governments, therefore, can perform only the functions that the Diet chooses to delegate to them.

　新憲法は、アメリカ合衆国におけるような連邦制度、あるいは、1949年に連合国が西ドイツに対して設けるよう主張したような連邦制度は、設けていない。とはいえ、地方公共団体の長とその議会の議員は、住民が選挙する（1946年までは、県知事は中央政府により任命されていた）。

改　正

　新憲法は、各議院の総議員の3分の2が改正案に賛成し、有権者の投票で過半数の承認が得られたときに、改正することができる。

The new basic law does not establish a federal system like that in the United States or that which the Allies insisted be established in West Germany in 1949. However, local chief executives and the members of local government assemblies are popularly elected. (Before 1947, prefectural governors were appointed by the central government.)

Amendments

The new constitution may be amended when two-thirds of the members of each house vote for the proposed amendment and it is approved by a majority of the voters.

| 第3章 | 新憲法の適用と憲法改正運動 |

新憲法の適用

　新憲法は103条からなり、全76条の明治憲法とは対照的である。

　明治憲法は、神権的な天皇主権説に基づいていたが、国のそれぞれの機関の具体的な機能と相互の関係については新憲法ほど明確でなく、きわめて弾力的に適用することができた。このため、日本の政治制度は1920年代には寡頭政治から議会制民主政治へと発展し、1930年代には軍部に牛耳られることになった。

　新憲法は国民主権の原理を宣言するだけでなく、この原理が実際にどのように適用されるかをある程度細かく説明している。例えば、選挙で選ばれた国民の代表者に対して、内閣がどのように責任を負うのかが定められている。議院内閣制の民主主義は、旧憲法下でも確かに可能だった。しかし、それは新憲法下でのように、法的に保障されたものでは決してなかったのである。

　新憲法が施行される直前直後（1947年の1月から1948年の7月の間）に、国会は新憲法の規定を実施するために45の法律を可決した。これらの法律は、官僚、国会議員、GHQスタッフの緊密な協力で起草されたものであり、憲法立

Meiji Constitution
High school students join in celebrating the Meiji Constitution (1889).

| CHAPTER 3 | THE NEW CONSTITUTION IN PRACTICE AND THE REVISION MOVEMENT |

The New Constitution in Practice

The new constitution consists of 103 articles, contrasted with the 76 articles of the Meiji Constitution.

The Meiji document, although enunciating the theory of the divine-right sovereignty of the emperor, was less clear than the new constitution concerning the specific functions and mutual relationships of the organs of the state and could be applied very flexibly. Thus in the 1920s Japan's political system evolved from an oligarchy toward parliamentary democracy and in the 1930s became dominated by the military.

The new basic law not only declares the principle of popular sovereignty but also spells out in some detail how this principle is applied in practice; how, for example, the cabinet is answerable to the people's elected representatives. Although the parliamentary-cabinet system of democracy was certainly possible under the old constitution, it was by no means legally assured, as is the case under the new basic law.

Shortly before and after the new constitution became effective (between January 1947 and July 1948), the Diet passed 45 laws to implement the provisions of the new constitution. As these laws were drafted by bureaucrats, Diet members, and SCAP officials

案者の意図をかなり正確に反映していると言ってよい。

　憲法を実施するこれらの法律の中には、新しい皇室典範、内閣法、国会法、財政法、労働基準法、裁判所法、検察庁法、地方自治法、国家公務員法、警察官職務執行法、内務省廃止法、法務庁設置法、選挙諸法、民法と民事訴訟法の改正、人身保護法などがある。

　このように、新憲法の規定は法律体系全体のすみずみにまで流れており、その効力が簡単に損なわれることはないだろう。

憲法改正運動

　1952年に占領が終わると、連合国の支持で進められた様々な改革への民族主義的な反動が起こり、その一つとして保守両党（自由党と改進党）に憲法改正の運動が起きた。

Takayanagi Kenzō
Chairman of the
Commission on
the Constitution
(1957–65)

　1956年、保守が支配する国会は、新憲法の起源・運用・考えられる改正点を調査するため、憲法調査会をつくる法律を可決した。

　こうした憲法改正運動は、労働組合の連合体である総評、日本共産党、日本社会党などに後押しされた憲法擁護国民連合の激しい反対にあ

in close collaboration, they may be said to reflect fairly accurately the intent of the framers of the constitution.

The implementing legislation included the new Imperial Household Law, the Cabinet Law, the Diet Law, the Finance Law, the Labor Standards Law, the Court Organization Law, the Public Prosecutors' Office Law, the Local Autonomy Law, the Civil Service Law, the Police Law, the Law Abolishing the Home Ministry, the Law Creating the Attorney-General's Office, electoral laws, amendments to the Civil Code and Code of Civil Procedure, and a Habeas Corpus Law.

Thus the provisions of the new constitution permeate the entire legal system and will not easily be reduced to ineffectiveness.

The Constitution Revision Movement

With the end of the Occupation in 1952, a movement to amend the constitution arose in both conservative parties (the Liberal Party and the *Kaishintō*) as part of a nationalistic reaction against the Allied-sponsored reforms.

In 1956 the conservative-controlled Diet passed a law creating the Commission on the Constitution to study the origins of the new constitution, its operation, and its possible amendment.

The constitution revision movement was vigorously opposed by the People's League to Protect the Constitution, backed by the labor federation *Sōhyō*, the Japan

った。1960年代になると、自由民主党は選挙での支持をしだいに失った。憲法改正を発議するために必要な、国会の両院での3分の2の多数を制する、という自民党の望みが遠ざかるにつれ、憲法改正運動は勢いを失った。

　外国人の手で起草されたという弱味はあるとしても、新憲法ははじめから日本の自由主義者や革新的な人々の支持を得てきた。女性、学者、労働組合員、ジャーナリスト、宗教的・民族的マイノリティなど、新たに選挙権を与えられたり解放された人々は、憲法によって保障された自由の価値を理解して尊重するようになった。そして、保守勢力からの実際の攻撃、あるいは攻撃のように思えたものから憲法を守ろうとするようになった。

　1946年の制定以来、憲法の改正は国会の両院のどちらからも提案されたことはなく、提案された改正を国民投票にかけるための手続きを具体的に決める法律は、まだ何も可決されたことがない。

Communist Party, and the Japan Socialist Party. As the Liberal-Democrats gradually lost electoral support in the 1960s and their hopes receded for control of the two-thirds majorities in both houses of the Diet necessary to initiate constitutional amendments, the constitution revision movement lost its impetus.

Notwithstanding the taint of foreign authorship, the new constitution has enjoyed from the beginning the support of liberals and progressives in Japan. Newly enfranchised or liberated groups, including women, academicians, labor unionists, journalists, and religious and ethnic minorities, have come to understand and cherish their constitutionally guaranteed freedoms and to defend the basic law against real or imagined attacks by conservatives.

Since its enactment in 1946, no constitutional amendment has been proposed by either house of the Diet, nor has any law yet been passed specifying the procedure for a popular vote on a proposed amendment.

ビジュアル 英語で読む日本国憲法
The Constitution of Japan

1997年5月9日　第1刷発行

編　者　　講談社インターナショナル株式会社

発行者　　野間佐和子

発行所　　講談社インターナショナル株式会社
　　　　　〒112　東京都文京区音羽1-17-14
　　　　　電話　03-3944-6493（編集）
　　　　　　　　03-3944-6492（営業）

印刷所　　大日本印刷株式会社

製本所　　株式会社 堅省堂

落丁本・乱丁本は、講談社インターナショナル営業局宛にお送りください。送料小社負担にてお取替えいたします。なお、この本についてのお問い合わせは、編集局第2出版部宛にお願いいたします。本書の無断複写（コピー）は著作権法上での例外を除き、禁じられています。

定価はカバーに表示してあります。

英語で読んでも面白い!

1 楽しく読めて自然に英語が身に付くバイリンガル表記
2 実用から娯楽まで読者の興味に応える多彩なテーマ
3 重要単語、表現法が一目で分かる段落対応レイアウト

英語で話す「日本」Q&A

Talking About Japan Q & A   ISBN 4-7700-2026-0

講談社インターナショナル [編]

外国の人と話すとき、必ず出てくる話題は「日本」のこと。でも英語力よりも前に困るのは、日本について知らないことがいっぱいという事実です。モヤモヤの知識をスッキリさせてくれる「日本再発見」の書。

英語で読む日本史

Japanese History: 11 Experts Reflect on the Past   ISBN 4-7700-2024-4

「英文日本大事典」[編]

11人の超一流ジャパノロジストたちが英語で書き下ろした日本全史。外国人の目から見た日本史はどういうものか、また、日本の歴史事項を英語で何と表現するのか。新しい視点が想像力をかき立てます。

英語で話す「日本の謎」Q&A

100 Tough Questions for Japan   ISBN 4-7700-2091-0

板坂 元 [監修]

なぜ、結婚式は教会で、葬式はお寺でなんてことができるの? なぜ、大人までがマンガを読むの? なぜ、時間とお金をかけてお茶を飲む練習をするの?──こんな外国人の問いをつきつめてゆくと、日本文化の核心が見えてきます。

英語で話す「日本の心」

Keys to the Japanese Heart and Soul   ISBN 4-7700-2082-1

「英文日本大事典」[編]

一流のジャパノロジスト53人が解説した「日本の心」を知るためのキーワード集。「わび」「さび」「義理人情」「甘え」「根回し」「談合」「禊」「穢れ」など、日本人特有の「心の動き」を外国人に説明するための強力なツールです。

ニッポン不思議発見!

Discover Japan: Words, Customs and Concept   ISBN 4-7700-2142-9

日本文化研究所 [編]   松本道弘 [訳]

絶望的な場合ですら、日本人は「そこをなんとか」という言葉を使って、相手に甘えようとするらしい……このような指摘をうけると、いかに日本人は独特なものの考え方をしているか分かります。あなたも"不思議"を発見してみませんか。

ニッポン見聞録
Heisei Highs and Lows
ISBN 4-7700-2092-9

トム・リード［著］

国際化の進む日本ですが、アメリカのジャーナリストが鋭い目と耳で浮き彫りにしたニッポンの姿は、驚くほど平穏で愛おしく、恥ずかしいくらい強欲で無知なものでした。トムが大好きな日本人へ贈る新・開国論。

「Japan」クリッピング
Views of Japan from The Washington Post Newsroom
ISBN 4-7700-2023-6

東郷茂彦［著］

アメリカの世論をリードするワシントン・ポストに書かれた「Japan」……政治、外交、経済、社会のジャンルで取り上げられた日本の姿を、国際ジャーナリストが解説し、その背後にある問題点を浮き彫りにする一冊。

英語で折り紙
Origami in English
ISBN 4-7700-2027-9

山口　真［著］

たった一枚の紙から無数の造形が生まれ出る……外国の人たちは、その面白さに目を見張ります。折るとき、英語で説明できるようにバイリンガルにしました。ホームステイ、留学、海外駐在に必携の一冊です。

英語で日本料理
100 Recipes from Japanese Cooking
ISBN 4-7700-2079-1

辻調理師専門学校　畑耕一郎, 近藤一樹［著］

外国の人と親しくなる最高の手段は、日本料理を作ってあげること、そしてその作り方を教えてあげることです。代表的な日本料理100品の作り方を、外国の計量法も入れながら、バイリンガルで分かりやすく解説しました。

アメリカ日常生活のマナーQ&A
Do As Americans Do
ISBN 4-7700-2128-3

ジェームス・M・バーダマン／倫子・バーダマン［著］

"How do you do?" に "How do you do?" と答えてはいけないということ、ご存知でしたか？　日本では当たり前と思われていたことがマナー違反だったのです。旅行で、駐在で、留学でアメリカに行く人必携のマナー集。

日米比較・冠婚葬祭のマナー
Do It Right: Japanese & American Social Etiquette
ISBN 4-7700-2025-2

ジェームス・M・バーダマン／倫子・バーダマン［著］

アメリカでは結婚式や葬式はどのように行われるのか？　お祝いや香典は？……そしてアメリカの人たちも、日本の事情を知りたがります。これだけあればもう困らない。日米冠婚葬祭マニュアル、バイリンガル版。